FRESH SPANISH

SERGIO VASQUEZ

hamlyn

**TO DELIA TARTERA COLL AND
NURIA MARTINEZ TARTERA, WITH
THANKS FOR ALL THEIR HELP IN
THIS PROJECT**

An Hachette Livre UK Company

First published in Great Britain in 2008 by
Hamlyn, a division of Octopus Publishing Group Ltd
2–4 Heron Quays, London E14 4JP
www.octopusbooks.co.uk

Copyright © Octopus Publishing Group Ltd 2008

The material in this book was previously published
in *Fresh Spanish*

ISBN: 978-0-600-61779-2

A CIP catalogue record for this book is available
from the British Library

Printed and bound in China

10 9 8 7 6 5 4 3 2 1

NOTE

Both metric and imperial measurements have been given in all
recipes. Use one set of measurements only, and not a mixture
of both.

Standard level spoon measurements are used in all recipes.
1 tablespoon = one 15 ml spoon
1 teaspoon = one 5 ml spoon

Ovens should be preheated to the specified temperature – if
using a fan-assisted oven, follow the manufacturer's
instructions for adjusting the time and the temperature.

Fresh herbs should be used unless otherwise stated.

Medium eggs should be used unless otherwise stated.

The Department of Health advises that eggs should not be
consumed raw. This book contains some dishes made with raw
or lightly cooked eggs. It is prudent for vulnerable people such
as pregnant and nursing mothers, invalids, the elderly, babies
and young children to avoid uncooked or lightly cooked dishes
made with eggs. Once prepared, these dishes should be kept
refrigerated and used promptly.

This book includes dishes made with nuts and nut derivatives.
It is advisable for those with known allergic reactions to nuts
and nut derivatives and those who may be potentially
vulnerable to these allergies, such as pregnant and nursing
mothers, invalids, the elderly, babies and children, to avoid
dishes made with nuts and nut oils. It is also prudent to check
the labels of pre-prepared ingredients for the possible inclusion
of nut derivatives.

CONTENTS

INTRODUCTION

Spanish cooking enjoys the full benefit of the vibrant flavours and health-promoting properties for which the Mediterranean diet is famed. Spain's cuisine is based on an abundant supply of quality local produce – from luscious sun-ripened tomatoes and sweet peppers to juicy oranges, peaches and figs; from expertly produced meats and freshly hauled fish to an array of cheeses. The cooking is characterized by a unique, distinctive mix of flavours, enriched by complex historical influences as well as special techniques and a particular approach to eating. This book taps into the best that Spanish cuisine has to offer, celebrating its approach to food as a laid-back, joyful and healthy way of life.

Spanish cuisine is rich with the country's history, displaying the multicultural influences of a varied past. The Moors from North Africa, who spent some 800 years in Spain, brought with them their favourite foods and flavourings such as almonds, aubergines, cinnamon, cumin, nutmeg and honey, as well as culinary techniques such as cooking meat on skewers over an open fire, frying in olive oil and preserving in vinegar. The Spanish words for rice, *arroz*, oil, *aceite*, and almonds, *almendras*, are all Arabic in origin.

The Jewish community, which settled in Spain over several centuries, also left its mark on various classic Spanish dishes. Not least of these is *cocido (see page 156)*, Spain's national dish of slow-simmered meat, vegetables and chickpeas, which closely resembles *dafina*, the Sabbath stew of the Sephardi Jews.

Catholicism, too, has had a significant influence on Spanish cuisine. Salt cod, which plays such a key role in Spanish cooking, was preserved for fast days, and pork became an integral part of the cuisine simply because it had been forbidden by both the Moors and Jews who were subsequently ejected from the country. During the time of the Spanish Inquisition, eating pork became a proof of loyalty to the Catholic Church.

Added to these religious influences, there are of course regional influences in Spanish cooking, with the plains, mountains and sea offering a wonderful variety of produce. Each region makes the most of its natural wealth, giving a unique character to the cuisine of that area. Along the Pyrenees lie the Basque country, Navarre and Aragon, each with its own distinctive cooking. In the Basque country you will find fabulous seafood from both the Mediterranean and Atlantic – and salt cod is big business. From Navarre comes a bounty of wonderful vegetables and from Aragon's mountains a wealth of game. In the north, Galicia is frequently referred to as the seafood province, while Asturias is

known for its hearty bean and sausage dishes, including the famous *fabada*, as well as its superior cheeses.

In central Spain – Madrid, northern Castile and Leon, New Castile, La Mancha and Extremadura – you will find food with strong, robust flavours, with roast pork and lamb, slow-simmered stews and flavourful vegetable dishes being common fare. Extremadura is particularly well known for its premium pigs and of course the resulting hams, sausages and pâtés.

Andalusia in the south exhibits a noticeable Arab influence in its cuisine, as does its architecture, agriculture, music and gardening. Its most famous foods are its green olives and red dried hams, but fish and seafood are also a draw. The area has a thriving agriculture, growing a rich variety of fruit and vegetables.

Catalonia and Levante lie along the east coast. The Catalan cuisine reveals French influences, and serves up wonderful fish and seafood dishes. Rustic meals using beans and sausages are popular, too. Levante is home to Valencia, the birthplace of what may be Spain's most famous dish, paella – but there are also many other wonderful rice dishes to sample. Together, the regions of Spain offer perhaps the most varied array of nourishing and delicious dishes to be found in any one national cuisine.

EATING SPANISH STYLE

Spanish life revolves around food, beginning with breakfast eaten in a bar on the way to work, followed by a long, leisurely lunch consumed around 2 pm, then a snack after work and ending with a supper late in the evening. Meals are seen as a time for coming together and socializing, but it is not just full-blown meals that offer the opportunity for social interaction. Tapas – that most valued of Spanish inventions – is the perfect way to get together informally with friends and catch up over a drink and a light bite. It all began in Andalusia, and the legend goes that a slice of bread or cheese was placed over a glass to keep off the flies (the Spanish word *tapa* means 'cover'). The tradition spread and you will find tapas bars all over Spain, filled with people chatting, drinking and eating. Like all Spanish food, tapas make the most of fresh local ingredients and vary according to season and region. The tapas themselves range from the lightest nibbles, such as delicious marinated olives *(see page 58)*, to more substantial snacks such as the classic potato and tomato dish, *patatas bravas (see page 68)*, and meatballs *(albóndigas)* in a spiced tomato sauce *(see page 28)*.

Fiestas and celebrations, too, are a time for eating and drinking. There are special foods for feast days, and every town has its own fiesta in which people gather to celebrate, eat and drink. Literally thousands of these fiestas take place across the country in a single year.

HEALTHY EATING While the variety, freshness and quality of the ingredients used in Spanish cooking naturally create a nutritious and well-balanced diet, all the recipes in this book have been specially selected and crafted with health in mind. For example, unsaturated fats have been chosen in preference to saturated ones. Unsaturated fats, such as the olive oil that plays such an important role in Spanish cuisine, help to increase the ratio of 'good' cholesterol (which is carried in the blood by high-density lipoproteins or HDL) to 'bad' cholesterol (which is carried in the blood by the low-density lipoproteins or LDL). In contrast, saturated fats, such as butter, increase the blood's quantity of 'bad' LDL cholesterol, which is associated with increased risk of cardiovascular disease.

It's well known that eating too much salt can raise blood pressure, potentially leading to heart disease and stroke. Fortunately, Spanish cooking is rich in delicious, healthy flavourings, such as fresh Mediterranean herbs, spices and aromatics. The amount of added salt in the recipes has been reduced in favour of sprinklings of fresh herbs such as parsley, tarragon and mint, spices such as pimentón, cinnamon and saffron, and healthy flavourings such as garlic and lemon juice.

The generous use of fresh, seasonal vegetables is one of the joys of the Spanish table, as well as one of the

reasons why the cuisine is so good for you. These recipes feature a wide range of fresh vegetables, incorporating them both raw and cooked to make the most of their fabulous colours, flavours and textures. Also liberally included in the recipes is fresh fruit. In Spain, fruit is used in both sweet and savoury dishes – oranges, for example, which are a brilliant source of vitamin C, are frequently cooked with chicken and fish and are also often used in desserts *(see pages 158 and 244)*.

For the meat and poultry recipes, it is the low-fat cuts that have been chosen. There are also plenty of dishes featuring oily fish, such as sardines, mackerel and clams, which contain the essential omega-3 fatty acids that are considered so important for good health.

The recipes in this book also major on the healthy cooking techniques prevalent in the Spanish cuisine –

steaming, braising, grilling, baking and shallow-frying in a minimum of oil. Less healthy techniques traditionally used in some classic recipes have been replaced with a healthier yet equally tasty option. For example, salt cod cakes, which are usually fried, are instead brushed with oil and baked *(see page 44)*.

FRESH INGREDIENTS

From the mountains, plains and seas of Spain comes a wealth of fresh ingredients – luscious fruit and ripe vegetables, creamy cheeses, fish and seafood, and top-quality meats, cured and fresh. Good meat is valued in Spain, a country where purely vegetarian cooking is virtually unknown. However, vegetables are just as essential and many dishes are light on meat – you will often find that just a little chorizo has been added to a vegetable-based dish, for example. Freshly-caught fish and seafood also play a huge role, thanks to Spain's two long coastlines – one bordering the Atlantic and the other the Mediterranean. With the fabulous quality of ingredients, little adornment is necessary and fish and seafood are frequently cooked simply – boiled or grilled over an open fire.

VEGETABLES The warm climate is perfect for growing plump tomatoes, peppery chillies, sweet juicy peppers and shiny fat aubergines – all of which contribute a vibrant, typically Mediterranean flavour to the cuisine. Onions and garlic are also central to Spanish cooking, while leafy cabbages and tender spinach are beloved across the country. Potatoes, of course, are essential for that classic tapas dish, *patatas bravas (see page 68)*, and they are also added to stews and served as an accompaniment. Another favourite root is the turnip, which is particularly popular in Galicia. Wild mushrooms are a cherished ingredient, and are picked throughout the year, particularly in Catalonia and the Basque country. Vegetables are cooked in many ways: served in tapas like *tomates rellenos* (Stuffed Tomatoes, *see page 72*) and *pimientos fritos* (Sautéed Sweet Green Peppers, *see page 62*), added to eggs, or cooked with meat or fish, to name but a few.

HERBS These natural flavourings play an important role in the Spanish kitchen. Robust herbs such as rosemary, thyme, oregano and bay are used in meat and bean stews, while tender, fragrant fennel is popularly used with seafood and flat leaf parsley is generously added to all manner of savoury dishes.

PORK Pork is one of Spain's most popular meats, not least because of its significance in the country's religious past *(see page 6)*. All families would once have owned a pig, to be fattened up before slaughter and then cured and made into sausages. Of all Spain's sausages, chorizo – spiced and coloured red with paprika – is the most widely known. It may be fried, boiled or added to stews, while the cured sausage can be thinly sliced and served on bread as a tapa. Spain produces some of Europe's finest hams, and about one-fifth of the country's pigs are bred for this purpose. *Jamón Serrano* or Serrano ham – named after the Sierra mountains – is one of the most famous. The sweet hams are highly prized and cured with less salt than those produced further south. Fresh pork is also widely used: grilled, added to stews or made into skewers.

BEEF The Spanish have never been great beef eaters, preferring to reserve their bulls for fighting, but veal is popular. Unlike in other parts of Europe, Spanish veal is not intensively reared. It is braised, pan-fried or minced and made into meatballs such as *albóndigas (see page 28)*.

LAMB This is traditionally eaten in mountain and grazing regions, and is a classic Easter and wedding treat in other parts of Spain. Chops may be grilled and the legs braised or roasted, while other cuts may be stewed in classic dishes such as Lamb with Lemon and Garlic *(see page 162)*.

GAME Wild rabbits thrive across Spain. They form the basis of many stews and braised dishes, and different regions have their own specialities. Wild duck can be found on the lakes and salt flats, and duck shooting is a popular sport. The birds are frequently braised, and often paired with fruit such as oranges and pears. There are literally millions of tiny quail that fly across the country and they make wonderful eating – roasted or casseroled and often cooked with fruit such as sultanas or grapes *(see page 154)*.

CHICKEN A favourite throughout the country, there are many regional chicken dishes whose flavouring reflects the area in which the birds are reared. Chicken may be roasted, braised and stewed, and is frequently teamed with red peppers, oranges, chickpeas or rice, and flavoured with paprika. Sherry or red wine may also be used, according to the region.

FISH Tuna are fished off Gibraltar in the *alamadraba*, an ancient tradition in which men fight the huge fish in the sea. The flesh may be grilled, braised or stewed and is traditionally used in the fish and potato stew, *marmita-kua (see page 220)*. Mackerel are fished locally and cooked simply, or stewed or pickled in vinegar, as in the

Moorish dish *caballa en escabeche (see page 208)*. Sardines are enjoyed in all the coastal regions. On the Malaga coast, the *moraga* festival marks the beginning of summer, when sardines are skewered on sticks and cooked over open fires on the beach.

PRAWNS These are fished on both coasts and several different types are used in the Spanish kitchen. Tiny *camarones* and small Mediterranean prawns are stirred into numerous dishes and cooked in fritters, while larger pink *gambas* are used in tapas classics such as *gambas al ajillo (see page 26)* and *gambas con romesco (see page 50)*. The larger scampi or tiger prawns, which have a wonderful flavour, are perfect for adding to salads.

CRAB This is a delicacy in the coastal regions, particularly on the north coast. Crabs are often boiled and served in their shells, or baked and dressed as in the classic Basque dish *txangurro al horno (see page 218)*. *Txangurro* is the Basque name for the giant spider or spiny crabs that are traditionally used in the dish, which can weigh up to 2.25 kg (5 lb) or more.

SCALLOPS These are the emblem of Santiago de Compostela and famous in Galicia, where you will find glorious sweet, juicy specimens, large and small. They may be cooked in wine or a tomato sauce, fried or topped with breadcrumbs or grilled as in the wonderful *vieiras de Vigo (see page 214)*.

MUSSELS Galicia and Tarragona are important areas for mussels, where they are grown on ropes. Many are canned, but fresh ones are also enjoyed – topped with garlic and breadcrumbs and grilled as a tapa, steamed open in wine or added to fish stews such as the classic *zarzuela (see page 224)*.

CLAMS Juicy clams are found in countless dishes, from simple tapas with wine, tomatoes and herbs to hearty pasta and rice dishes such as *arroz con almejas y vegetales (see page 198)*. They are gathered on both coasts and vary in size.

SQUID AND OCTOPUS Squid is often cooked very quickly until just tender: deep-fried in batter, pan-fried or griddled as in *calamares a la parilla (see page 48)*. It may also be stuffed and simmered slowly in dishes such

as *calamares rellenos (see page 212)*. Octopus suits long, slow simmering and is wonderful in simple dishes such as Galician-style *pulpo a la Gallega (see page 43)* or stews.

CHEESES Spain produces several hundred distinctively flavoured cheeses, many regional, from cows', goats' and sheeps' milk. Manchego, made from sheep's milk, is probably the best known. Made in 3 kg (6½ lb) drums and pressed into grass moulds, which give the cheese its very distinctive patterned rind, it may be sold *semicurado* (under 13 weeks), *curado* (up to 6 months) and *viejo* (over 6 months). The flavour becomes more pronounced with age, with the *curado* bearing similarities to Italian Parmesan.

FRUIT A wonderful selection of fruit thrives in the Spanish climate, from sweet plump apricots to fragrant melons to zesty oranges. Tropical fruits such as kiwi fruit and passion fruit are also grown. Simple fresh fruit is a popular dessert, but desserts may also created by poaching peaches in wine *(see page 230)* or turning oranges into fruity ices *(see page 244)*.

THE SPANISH LARDER

The Spanish storecupboard is a rich, varied source of ingredients for pairing with fresh produce to create an authentic Spanish flavour.

OLIVES AND OLIVE OIL Cultivated in Spain for many millennia, the fruit of the olive tree is one of the joys of Spanish cooking. The fruit is either cured in brine for eating (they are inedible raw) or pressed to extract their rich greenish-gold oil. Olives are marinated and served as a tapa *(see page 58)*, while the oil – with its healthy unsaturated fats – is used for frying, drizzling and dressings, and imparts a distinctive flavour to dishes.

SPICES The spices used in Spanish cooking have strong roots in the Moorish tradition. Golden saffron was introduced by the Moors and is widely used – in paella, chicken and seafood dishes, as well as in sweet cakes and desserts. The spice is grown in La Mancha and is harvested by hand – hence its high price. Other Moorish spices include coriander and cumin. *Pimentón* or paprika is an everyday spice, used in a similar way to black pepper, and may be mild *(dulce)*, mildly spiced with chilli *(picante)* or bittersweet *(agridulce)*. Cinnamon and nutmeg are also popular spices in sweet dishes.

RICE Famously grown in Valencia, where it was originally planted by the Moors hundreds of years ago, rice is also grown in Seville and Murcia. Spanish rice has short, fat grains, not dissimilar to Italian risotto rice. It is classically used in paella *(see page 170)*, but this isn't the only rice dish loved by the Spanish. The grain is also used in stuffings, fritters, oven-baked dishes and soupy stews.

PASTA Made in Andalusia and Catalonia, pasta has been a Spanish staple since the late 18th century. It is used in soups and served with sauces, as in the Catalan dish *fideos a la Catalana (see page 190)*, where the pasta is baked in a rich tomato and sausage sauce.

DRIED BEANS AND PULSES Cooked in hearty, rustic dishes; chickpeas, flageolet and cannellini beans, dried broad beans and lentils play an important role in Spanish cooking. With the addition of smoky, spicy chorizo, they make popular tapas dishes.

PRESERVED AND CANNED FISH Probably one of the most distinctive and best-loved preserved fish in Spanish cooking is salt cod, known as *bacalao*. Despite the abundance of fresh fish from the sea, *bacalao* is probably one of the most popular everyday fish eaten in Spain – used in stews, turned into fishcakes *(see page 44)*, served in salads *(see page 98)* and much more. The hard, board-like pieces of fish must be soaked for at least 24 hours before cooking, to soften and to remove much of the salt, but once prepared and cooked, it truly is one of the treats of the Spanish table. Canned fish include tuna, which is used in dishes such as the little stuffed pastries, empanadillas *(see page 34)*, served as a tapa, and stuffed eggs, huevos rellenos *(see page 52)*. Anchovies, which are also enjoyed fresh when in season, are also popular. Usually salted before canning in oil, they may also be brine-pickled or smoked.

EQUIPMENT

The basic pots and utensils are all you really need to achieve the routinely fabulous culinary results of the traditional Spanish kitchen. Much traditional cooking is done over an open wood or charcoal fire, but the same effects can be produced with a regular cooker. Below, the most useful items of Spanish cookware are listed (along with suggestions for everyday substitutes).

PAELLERA This is the classic pan used for cooking paella. Large and flat with two handles and a dimpled base, the paellera can range in size from quite small to huge for a large party. Choose a medium one, 26–28 cm (10¼–11 inches) in diameter, for cooking for four people. It is important to use the correct size of pan for even distribution of the heat – it should be large enough to hold the rice in a single layer. Otherwise, use a heavy-based, shallow flameproof casserole or a heavy-based frying pan or sauté pan of the same size.

PUCHERO This is a large pot for cooking stews. Depending on the region, the puchero may be earthenware and fat and round in shape, or it may be metal with looped handles. Instead, you can use a large, heavy-based flameproof casserole with a tight-fitting lid – see below – or a good-quality heavy-based saucepan.

CAZUELAS These classic Spanish earthenware dishes, glazed on the inside, are frequently round in shape, but may also be oval. Cazuelas make perfect oven-to-table cookware and can be used for everything from tapas to large casseroles. To avoid risk of cracking, season a cazuela before use by half-filling it with water and a little vinegar and boiling until evaporated and use a heat diffuser on the hob.

FLAMEPROOF CASSEROLE This really is a key item of equipment for stewing and braising. A casserole needs to have a heavy base, as well as a heavy, tight-fitting lid to prevent evaporation. These items come in stainless steel or heavy-duty earthenware.

NONSTICK FRYING PAN This is handy for limiting the amount of oil used when shallow frying. Choose a good-quality pan, which will last much longer than cheap varieties.

HEAVY-BASED GRIDDLE PAN This is ideal for cooking meat and fish, and even shellfish, without the need for additional cooking oil, and achieves a delicious char-grilled flavour and appearance. The ridged cast-iron variety is a good choice.

KITCHEN KNIVES A good-quality, large cook's knife is indispensable for preparing ingredients. A small paring knife is also useful for small ingredients, as is a small, serrated knife for cutting tomatoes and fruit.

PESTLE AND MORTAR To make aioli (garlic paste) and tomato paste in the traditional Spanish style, you can use a pestle and mortar instead of a food processor. This piece of equipment is also handy for processing small quantities of other foods.

PREPARING SEAFOOD

Since Spanish fish and seafood dishes feature fresh ingredients, you will need to know how to prepare them for cooking, although with some items, such as octopus, squid and scallops, you can ask your fish supplier to do the task for you.

MUSSELS AND CLAMS Scrub the mussels or clams thoroughly, discarding any with damaged shells or those that do not shut when firmly tapped. Pull out any beards that are attached to the mussels. Put them in a large bowl of cold water and leave to soak for 30 minutes, or 1 hour if large – as in the case of razor clams *(see page 198)*. Drain and use as directed.

OCTOPUS Cut between the head and tentacles of the octopus, just below the eyes. Push the 'beak' out of the head through the centre of the tentacles and discard. Cut the eyes from the head and discard. Clean the head section by slicing through one side, being careful not to damage the ink sac, and scrape out all the guts. Rinse thoroughly under cold running water, pat dry with kitchen paper and use as directed in the recipe.

PRAWNS To peel, pull off the head and legs, then peel away the shell on the body and tail. To devein, make a shallow cut down the centre back, then lift out the black intestinal tract with the tip of the knife and discard.

SARDINES These fish should be scaled and gutted before cooking. Gutting is easy to do: simply cut the head almost through the backbone and then twist, pulling the head towards you. The guts will come away with the head.

SCALLOPS To remove scallops from their shells, grip them firmly with one hand covered with a tea towel, insert a strong, short knife between the two shells and twist firmly to prise the shells apart. Remove and discard the flat, greyish fringe around the scallop, reserving the white flesh and orange coral. If visible, remove and discard the black intestinal tract from the side of the flesh.

SQUID Pull the head and tentacles from the body – the intestines will come away with the head. Remove the squid's wings (the flat pieces of flesh either side of the body), then remove and discard the speckled skin from the body. Remove the skin from the wings, too, if you are using them in the dish. Cut the tentacles from the head, leaving them in one piece, and discard the head and intestines (apart from the ink sac if you want to use the ink). Cut or push out and discard the beak. Remove and discard the transparent bone from the body. Rinse the body, wings and tentacles under cold running water, pat dry with kitchen paper and use as directed.

MENU PLANS

FAMILY LUNCH 1 FOR 4 PEOPLE

Spinach, Tomato and Pine Nut Flatbread *(see page 148)*

Spring Vegetable Stew *(see page 124)*

FAMILY LUNCH 2 FOR 4 PEOPLE

Chicken Soup with Lemon and Mint *(see page 96)*

Baked Eggs with Chorizo, Ham and Asparagus *(see page 186)*

FAMILY DINNER 1 FOR 4 PEOPLE

Chickpeas with Chorizo *(see page 54)*

Traditional Fish and Potato Stew *(see page 220)*

Spanish-style Green Beans *(see page 123)*

Blood Orange Ice Lollies *(see page 244)*

FAMILY DINNER 2 FOR 4 PEOPLE

Andalusian-style Salad *(see page 106)*

Catalan-style Noodles with Pork Sausages *(see page 190)*

Catalan-style Spinach *(see page 128)*

Cinnamon Ice Cream *(see page 238)*

SUNDAY LUNCH FOR 4–6 PEOPLE

Andalusian Gazpacho *(see page 92)*

Stuffed Roasted Chicken *(see page 166)*

Spring Vegetable Stew *(see page 124)*

Peaches in Wine *(see page 230)*

SUMMER AL FRESCO MEAL FOR 6–8 PEOPLE

Prawns in Garlic *(see page 26)*

Baked Salt Cod Cakes *(see page 44)*

Potatoes with Tomatoes *(see page 68)*

Andalusian-style Salad *(see page 106)*

Peach and Lettuce Salad *(see page 105)*

Chilled White Almond and Grape Soup *(see page 90)*

Broad Beans with Ham *(see page 131)*

Almond and Lemon Cake *(see page 240)*

LARGE INFORMAL GATHERING FOR 8–10 PEOPLE

Stuffed Tomatoes *(see page 72)*

Tuna Turnovers *(see page 34)*

Garlic Mushrooms *(see page 42)*

Potatoes with Tomatoes *(see page 68)*

Anchovies with Grilled Red Peppers *(see page 60)*

Savoury Meatballs *(see page 28)*

Rice and Olive Salad *(see page 103)*

Almond and Lemon Cake *(see page 240)*

Stuffed Figs *(see page 236)*

Sparkling Peach Sangria *(see page 250)*

DINNER PARTY FOR 4 PEOPLE

Chilled White Almond and Grape Soup *(see page 90)*

Spanish Rice with Clams and Vegetables *(see page 198)*

Grilled Red Pepper Salad *(see page 104)*

Spanish Custard Creams *(see page 232)*

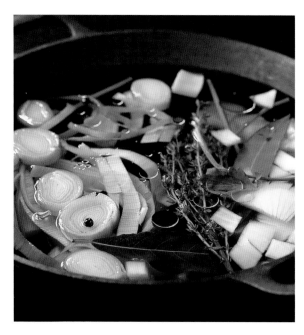

STOCKS

Homemade Spanish stocks do not vary greatly from the stocks used in other Mediterranean cuisines. A good stock needs good ingredients. Vegetables should be scrubbed of all clinging grit and fish bones should be thoroughly rinsed to remove any traces of blood. Chicken carcasses should be trimmed of excess fat. The length of cooking time for various stocks is of prime importance. An overcooked vegetable stock will be bland and tasteless, while an overcooked fish stock will be bitter. The opposite is true for meat stocks, as the longer cooking time enriches their flavour. These stocks can be made and, once cooled, frozen for later use. Try freezing in ice-cube trays for smaller portions.

VEGETABLE STOCK

INGREDIENTS 2 onions, finely chopped | 2 leeks, trimmed, cleaned and finely chopped | 8 celery sticks, finely chopped | 1 fennel bulb, trimmed and finely chopped | 2 large carrots, finely chopped | 2 bay leaves | 2 thyme sprigs | 2 flat leaf parsley sprigs | 1 rosemary sprig | ½ head of garlic, cut horizontally | 1 teaspoon black peppercorns | 3 litres (5¼ pints) cold water

ONE Put all the ingredients in a heavy-based saucepan and cover them with the measurement water. Bring to the boil, then reduce the heat and simmer gently, uncovered, for 45 minutes. **TWO** Leave to cool slightly before straining through a fine sieve. Leave to cool completely, then store in an airtight container in the refrigerator for up to 1 week or freeze for up to 1 month.

Makes about 2 litres (3½ pints)

CHICKEN STOCK

INGREDIENTS 2 chicken carcasses, about 2 kg (4 lb) in total | 1.5 litres (2½ pints) cold water | 1 onion, quartered | 1 turnip, roughly chopped | 1 large carrot, cut into thirds | a small bundle of fresh herbs, such as bay leaf, rosemary, thyme and flat leaf parsley | 1 teaspoon black peppercorns

ONE Put the chicken carcasses in a heavy-based saucepan, cover with the measurement water and bring to the boil. Add the vegetables, herbs and peppercorns, then reduce the heat, cover and simmer gently for 2½ hours. **TWO** Leave to cool slightly before straining through a fine sieve. Leave to cool completely, then store in an airtight container in the refrigerator for up to 2 days or freeze for up to 1 month. Before using the stock, remove and discard any surface fat.

Makes about 1 litre (1¾ pints)

FISH STOCK

INGREDIENTS 1 onion, finely chopped | 1 leek, trimmed, cleaned and finely chopped | 4 celery sticks, finely chopped | 1 kg (2 lb) very fresh fish bones, rinsed and cut into large pieces | 2 bay leaves | 2 dill sprigs | a few chervil sprigs | 1 teaspoon white peppercorns | ½ 75 cl (1¼ pint) bottle dry white wine | 1.5 litres (2½ pints) cold water | ice cubes

ONE Put half the vegetables in a wide, heavy-based saucepan and spread the fish bones over the top. Cover with the remaining vegetables, herbs and peppercorns. Add the wine and cover with the measurement water. Bring to the boil, then reduce the heat and simmer gently, uncovered, for 30 minutes, skimming off any scum that rises to the surface frequently and thoroughly. **TWO** Strain through a fine sieve and cool quickly over a bowl of ice. Store in an airtight container in the refrigerator for up to 1 week or freeze for up to 1 month.

Makes about 1 litre (1¾ pints)

TAPAS

PRAWNS IN GARLIC

This is the all-time favourite of tapas bars all over Spain. Fresh crab is sometimes used instead of prawns in the coastal towns and villages. Serve with crusty bread for mopping up the juices.

INGREDIENTS 250 g (8 oz) small raw prawns │ 3 tablespoons olive oil │ 2 garlic cloves, thinly sliced │ 2–3 small dried red chillies, crumbled │ salt

ONE Peel the prawns, leaving the tails intact, then devein *(see page 16)*. Pat them dry with kitchen paper. **TWO** Heat the oil in a medium *cazuela (see page 15)* over a heat diffuser or heat a shallow, flameproof casserole, add the garlic, chillies and prawns and cook over a medium-high heat, stirring, for 2–3 minutes until the prawns turn pink and are just cooked through. **THREE** Remove from the heat and serve the prawns immediately in the dish or casserole.

Serves 4

NUTRIENT ANALYSIS PER SERVING 442 kJ – 107 kcal – 6 g protein – 1 g carbohydrate – 0 g sugars – 9 g fat – 1 g saturates – 0 g fibre – 60 mg sodium

HEALTHY TIP Prawns are low in fat, while olive oil is rich in beneficial monounsaturated fats. Garlic helps to build up the immune system and prevent the formation of blood clots.

SAVOURY MEATBALLS

Moorish in origin, these fragrantly spiced little meatballs are tossed in a paprika-flavoured tomato sauce to make another well-loved tapas bar standard. For a variation, replace half the quantity of pork with minced veal.

INGREDIENTS 300 g (10 oz) minced pork | 3 garlic cloves, crushed | 50 g (2 oz) dried white breadcrumbs | 1 teaspoon ground cumin | 1 teaspoon ground coriander | 1 teaspoon ground nutmeg | 1 teaspoon ground cinnamon | 2 tablespoons olive oil | salt and freshly ground black pepper

SAUCE 1 tablespoon olive oil | 1 small onion, finely chopped | 1 garlic clove, crushed | 400 g (13 oz) can chopped tomatoes | 1 teaspoon golden caster sugar | 1 teaspoon pimentón dulce (mild paprika) | 100 g (3½ oz) fresh or frozen peas

ONE Put the minced meat, garlic, breadcrumbs, spices and salt and pepper to taste in a bowl and, using your fingers, mix together until the mixture is well combined. Cover and chill in the refrigerator for 1 hour to allow the flavours to develop. **TWO** Meanwhile, to make the sauce, heat the oil in a large frying pan, add the onion and garlic and cook over a medium heat, stirring frequently, for 5–6 minutes. Stir in the tomatoes and their juice, sugar and pimentón and bring to the boil. Reduce the heat, cover and simmer gently, stirring occasionally, for 25–30 minutes. Add the peas, season to taste with salt and pepper and cook for 2–3 minutes. **THREE** Take walnut-sized pieces of the minced meat mixture and shape into balls. Heat half the oil in a nonstick frying pan, add half the balls and cook over a medium heat, stirring, for 2–3 minutes until browned all over. Remove with a slotted spoon and drain on kitchen paper. Repeat with the remaining oil and meatballs. **FOUR** Add the meatballs to the sauce over a medium heat, stir to coat evenly, then simmer gently for 5–6 minutes. Serve hot.

Makes about 30

NUTRIENT ANALYSIS PER SERVING 1122 kJ – 266 kcal – 20 g protein – 15 g carbohydrate – 6 g sugars – 15 g fat – 3 g saturates – 3 g fibre – 164 mg sodium

HEALTHY TIP If using frozen peas, try smaller varieties such as petit pois, as they contain more fibre than larger peas. Frozen peas may have more vitamin content than fresh peas, because they are frozen very soon after picking.

recipe illustrated on pages 30–31

CLAMS WITH TOMATOES

INGREDIENTS 2 tablespoons olive oil | 3 garlic cloves, finely chopped | 2 ripe tomatoes, finely chopped | 1 kg (2 lb) live clams, prepared *(see page 16)* | 125 ml (4 fl oz) Manzanilla sherry | 4 tablespoons finely chopped flat leaf parsley | salt and freshly ground black pepper

ONE Heat the oil in a large frying pan, add the garlic and tomatoes and cook, stirring, for 3–4 minutes. **TWO** Add the drained clams to the pan with the sherry and parsley. Season to taste with salt and pepper, then cover tightly and cook over a high heat, shaking the pan vigorously several times, for 4–5 minutes or until all the clams have opened (discard any that remain closed). **THREE** Serve the clams immediately in their cooking liquid or leave to cool to room temperature.

Serves 4

NUTRIENT ANALYSIS PER SERVING 660 kJ – 160 kcal – 11 g protein – 5 g carbohydrate – 3 g sugars – 7 g fat – 1 g saturates – 1 g fibre – 57 mg sodium

HEALTHY TIP Clams have quite a low fat content and a high proportion of this is present as omega-3 fatty acids, which help to protect against heart disease.

TUNA TURNOVERS

These small tapa turnovers, which are hugely popular in Spain, are usually deep-fried, but here they are baked until golden to reduce the fat content. You can vary the stuffing ingredients to use any cooked fish or vegetables of your choice.

INGREDIENTS 1 tablespoon olive oil | 2 tablespoons very finely chopped onion | 75 g (3 oz) cooked, flaked fresh tuna or drained and flaked canned tuna in spring water | 2 tablespoons finely chopped drained canned pimiento | 2 tablespoons finely chopped tomato | 1 tablespoon finely chopped flat leaf parsley | 2 tablespoons finely chopped hard-boiled egg | 2 tablespoons organic tomato ketchup | 250 g (8 oz) ready-made shortcrust pastry, defrosted if frozen | plain flour, for dusting | beaten egg, to glaze | salt and freshly ground black pepper

ONE To make the filling, heat the oil in a large, nonstick frying pan, add the onion and cook over a low heat, stirring occasionally, for 12–15 minutes until soft and golden. Add the tuna, pimiento, tomato and parsley and cook over a medium heat, stirring frequently, for 5 minutes. **TWO** Remove the pan from the heat, then add the egg and tomato ketchup and mix well. Season to taste with salt and pepper and leave to cool slightly. **THREE** Roll the pastry out thinly on a lightly floured work surface. Using a 7 cm (3 inch) round plain pastry cutter, stamp out 20 rounds, reusing the trimmings. Line 2 large baking sheets with nonstick baking paper and arrange 10 pastry rounds on each one. **FOUR** Put a heaped teaspoonful of the filling into the centre of each round and then fold over the pastry to form a turnover. Seal the edges with a fork or crimp with your fingers. Brush each turnover with beaten egg and bake in a preheated oven, 190°C (375°F), Gas Mark 5, for 12–15 minutes until golden brown and crisp. Serve warm or at room temperature.

Makes 20

NUTRIENT ANALYSIS PER SERVING 318 kJ – 76 kcal – 2 g protein – 7 g carbohydrate – 1 g sugars – 4 g fat – 1 g saturates – 1 g fibre – 100 mg sodium

HEALTHY TIP If it's difficult to find tuna canned in spring water, use tuna canned in brine and drain and rinse it before use. Alternatively, use tuna canned in oil and use the drained olive oil for cooking the onion and other ingredients.

recipe illustrated on pages 36–37

GRILLED MONKFISH AND CAPER SKEWERS

Grilled fish skewers such as these are found in many of the tapas bars in the coastal regions of Spain. Monkfish has been used here, but you could substitute other firm fish such as fresh tuna, swordfish or halibut if you prefer.

INGREDIENTS 400 g (13 oz) monkfish fillet, skinned │ finely grated rind of 1 lemon │ juice of ½ lemon │ 1 tablespoon olive oil, plus extra for oiling │ 16 large caperberries │ 8 pimiento-stuffed green olives │ salt and freshly ground black pepper

ONE Cut the monkfish into 24 evenly-sized pieces and put them in a non-reactive bowl. Mix the lemon rind and juice and oil together in a jug or small bowl. Pour over the monkfish and season to taste with salt and pepper. Cover with clingfilm and leave to marinate at room temperature for 10 minutes. **TWO** Using 8 bamboo skewers, presoaked in cold water for 30 minutes, or 8 metal ones, thread 3 pieces of monkfish, 2 caperberries and 1 olive alternately on to each skewer. **THREE** Arrange the skewers on a lightly oiled grill rack and cook under a preheated high grill for 3–4 minutes on each side or until the fish is just cooked through. Serve immediately.

Serves 4

NUTRIENT ANALYSIS PER SERVING 570 kJ – 133 kcal – 16 g protein – 1 g carbohydrate – 0 g sugars – 7 g fat – 1 g saturates – 1 g fibre – 975 mg sodium

HEALTHY TIP Canned or bottled capers and olives prepared in brine will have a high salt content. Rinsing them in water before use will help to reduce the level of sodium in the dish.

recipe illustrated on pages 40–41

GARLIC MUSHROOMS

INGREDIENTS 3 tablespoons olive oil │ 250 g (8 oz) large mushrooms, such as field or Portobello, trimmed and halved or quartered if very large │ 6 garlic cloves, finely chopped │ 4 tablespoons fino sherry │ 2 tablespoons lemon juice │ 1 teaspoon dried red chilli flakes │ a small handful of roughly chopped flat leaf parsley │ salt

ONE Heat the oil in a large, nonstick frying pan over a high heat and add the mushrooms, stirring constantly. Stir in the garlic, sherry, lemon juice and chilli flakes and season to taste with salt. Cook, stirring frequently, for 5–6 minutes. **TWO** Remove from the heat and sprinkle over the chopped parsley. Serve immediately.

Serves 4

NUTRIENT ANALYSIS PER SERVING 436 kJ – 105 kcal – 2 g protein – 1 g carbohydrate – 1 g sugars – 9 g fat – 1 g saturates – 2 g fibre – 13 mg sodium

HEALTHY TIP Mushrooms contain useful amounts of the trace mineral copper, essential for the healthy growth and repair of bones and connective tissue.

GALICIAN-STYLE OCTOPUS

INGREDIENTS 500 g (1 lb) baby octopus, prepared *(see page 16)* | 12 black peppercorns | 2 bay leaves | olive oil, for drizzling | pimentón dulce (mild paprika), for sprinkling | salt | chunky lemon wedges, to serve

ONE Bring a large saucepan of water to the boil over a high heat. Add the octopus, peppercorns and bay leaves and season to taste with salt. Return to the boil, then reduce the heat to low and simmer very gently, uncovered, for 2 hours or until the octopus is very tender, topping up the water if necessary. **TWO** Remove the octopus from the water, drain well and leave to rest for 10–12 minutes. Using a sharp knife, cut the tentacles into 1 cm (½ inch) thick slices and cut the head into small, bite-sized pieces. **THREE** Arrange the octopus on a wooden board and serve drizzled with a little oil, sprinkled with pimentón and with lemon wedges for squeezing over.

Serves 4

NUTRIENT ANALYSIS PER SERVING 458 kJ – 110 kcal – 17 g protein – 0 g carbohydrate – 0 g sugars – 4 g fat – 0 g saturates – 0 g fibre – 5 mg sodium

HEALTHY TIP Octopus is very low in fat. It also contains the trace mineral selenium, essential for the formation of thyroid hormones, as well as a useful amount of copper.

BAKED SALT COD CAKES

Usually deep-fried, these delectable morsels of salt cod and potato are baked for a healthier option. Salt cod was first brought to Spain by the Basque fishermen and is a national food. Serve with a fresh tomato sauce or reduced-fat mayonnaise, if you like.

INGREDIENTS 300 g (10 oz) salt cod │ 300 g (10 oz) mashed potatoes │ 4 spring onions, very finely chopped │ 2 garlic cloves, crushed │ 50 g (2 oz) self-raising flour │ 1 egg, lightly beaten │ 4 tablespoons finely chopped flat leaf parsley │ olive oil, for brushing │ freshly ground black pepper │ lemon wedges, to garnish

ONE Soak the salt cod in a bowl of cold water overnight, changing the water 3–4 times to remove the excess salt. Drain, put in a large saucepan, cover with fresh cold water and bring to the boil. Reduce the heat to very low and simmer very gently, uncovered, for 30–40 minutes or until the fish is tender. **TWO** Drain the fish, remove and discard the skin and bones and flake the flesh into a bowl. Add the mashed potatoes, spring onions, garlic, flour, egg and parsley to the fish and, using your fingers, mix together until well combined. Cover and chill in the refrigerator for 3–4 hours to allow the flavours to develop. **THREE** Line 1–2 baking sheets with nonstick baking paper. Shape the fish mixture into small, bite-sized balls or cakes and arrange on the prepared baking sheets. Lightly brush the cakes with oil. **FOUR** Bake in a preheated oven, 180°C (350°F), Gas Mark 4, for 15–20 minutes or until lightly browned. Serve hot from the oven, garnished with the lemon wedges.

Makes about 30

NUTRIENT ANALYSIS PER SERVING 1130 kJ – 267 kcal – 29 g protein – 22 g carbohydrate – 1 g sugars – 8 g fat – 3 g saturates – 2 g fibre – 398 mg sodium

HEALTHY TIP Thorough rinsing and draining will considerably reduce the amount of salt in the dish. Cod is low in fat, and fresh tomato sauce will have a lower fat content than even reduced-fat mayonnaise.

recipe illustrated on pages 46–47

GRIDDLED SQUID

INGREDIENTS 500 g (1 lb) prepared baby squid *(see page 16)* | 2 tablespoons olive oil, plus extra for oiling | finely grated rind and juice of 1 lemon | 2 garlic cloves, crushed | 2 tablespoons finely chopped flat leaf parsley | salt and freshly ground black pepper

ONE Put the squid, including the tentacles, in a shallow, non-reactive bowl. Mix the oil, lemon rind and juice, garlic and parsley together in a jug or small bowl. Pour over the squid and season to taste with salt and pepper. Cover with clingfilm and leave to marinate in the refrigerator for 30 minutes. **TWO** Preheat a grill until very hot or heat a heavy-based griddle pan over a high heat until smoking. Arrange the squid on a lightly oiled grill rack and cook under the grill, turning once, for 2–3 minutes or until just cooked and tender. Alternatively, cook the squid, in batches, in the griddle pan for 2–3 minutes. Remove from the pan and keep hot while cooking the remaining squid. Serve hot.

Serves 4

NUTRIENT ANALYSIS PER SERVING 700 kJ – 169 kcal – 19 g protein – 1 g carbohydrate – 0 g sugars – 9 g fat – 1 g saturates – 0 g fibre – 220 mg sodium

HEALTHY TIP Squid has a low fat content, most of which is monounsaturated. This sort of fat increases the ratio of 'good' HDL cholesterol to 'bad' LDL cholesterol in the blood.

GRILLED PRAWNS WITH ROMESCO SAUCE

Romesco is the classic sauce from Catalonia and is made from the famed romesco or nyora red pepper. In this case served with grilled prawns, the sauce also makes a great dip for vegetable crudités.

INGREDIENTS 20 large raw tiger prawns, peeled and deveined *(see page 16)*, with tails left intact

SAUCE 4 tablespoons olive oil, plus extra for brushing │ 50 g (2 oz) good-quality white bread, crusts removed │ 1 large red pepper, cored, deseeded and chopped │ 1 dried red chilli │ 250 g (8 oz) ripe tomatoes, chopped │ 4 garlic cloves, crushed │ 25 g (1 oz) ground almonds │ 50 ml (2 fl oz) red wine vinegar │ salt and freshly ground black pepper

ONE To make the sauce, heat the oil in a large frying pan over a medium-high heat. Break the bread into small pieces, add to the pan and fry, stirring, for 2–3 minutes until golden. Remove with a slotted spoon and drain on kitchen paper. **TWO** Add the red pepper, chilli, tomatoes and garlic to the pan and cook over a medium heat, stirring frequently, for 5–6 minutes. Remove and leave to cool. **THREE** Transfer the fried bread, red pepper mixture, ground almonds and vinegar to a blender or food processor. Season with salt and pepper, then blend until smooth, adding a little water if the mixture is too thick. Transfer to a bowl, cover and leave to stand at room temperature for 2–3 hours to allow the flavours to develop. **FOUR** Arrange the prawns on a grill rack and lightly brush with oil. Cook under a preheated high grill for 2–3 minutes on each side or until they turn pink and are just cooked through. Serve immediately with the sauce for dipping.

Serves 4

NUTRIENT ANALYSIS PER SERVING 934 kJ – 224 kcal – 11 g protein – 11 g carbohydrate – 5 g sugars – 15 g fat – 2 g saturates – 3 g fibre – 150 mg sodium

HEALTHY TIP Romesco sauce is an excellent source of vitamin C and carotene, both good antioxidants that may help prevent some forms of cancer and are essential to general wellbeing.

SPANISH-STYLE TUNA-STUFFED EGGS

Stuffed eggs are popular the world over and are loved by children and adults alike. These are quick and easy to prepare using canned tuna. You can make them with canned salmon if you prefer.

INGREDIENTS 4 hard-boiled eggs │ 100 g (3½ oz) can tuna in spring water, drained │ 2 tablespoons reduced-fat mayonnaise │ 1 tablespoon tomato purée │ pinch of pimentón dulce (mild paprika) │ salt

TO GARNISH finely chopped black olives │ chopped, drained canned pimiento │ finely chopped flat leaf parsley

ONE Shell the eggs, then halve lengthways. Using a teaspoon, carefully scoop out the yolks into a bowl. Put the egg white halves, cut-side up, on a serving plate and set aside. **TWO** Flake the tuna and add to the yolks with the mayonnaise, tomato purée and pimentón. Season to taste with salt and pepper and mix together until well combined. **THREE** Using a teaspoon, carefully spoon an equal quantity of the fish mixture into each egg white half. Lightly cover and chill in the refrigerator until ready to serve. **FOUR** Before serving, garnish with chopped black olives, pimiento and parsley.

Serves 4

NUTRIENT ANALYSIS PER SERVING 590 kJ – 140 kcal – 13 g protein – 2 g carbohydrate – 1 g sugars – 9 g fat – 2 g saturates – 0 g fibre – 228 mg sodium

HEALTHY TIP Eggs are a nourishing food, rich in protein, iron and vitamins A and D. They should not be eaten to excess, however, as the egg yolks are high in cholesterol.

CHICKPEAS WITH CHORIZO

Chickpeas are the most valued pulse in Spain. Unlike in the Middle East or India, where chickpeas are used in many forms such as in flour or pastes, the Spanish cook them from dried, after soaking, and then simply stew or boil them and eat them whole. In this hearty tapas dish, canned chickpeas, used for convenience, are cooked with spicy chorizo and ripe tomatoes. Serve with crusty bread.

INGREDIENTS 2 tablespoons olive oil | 1 red onion, finely chopped | 2 garlic cloves, crushed | 200 g (7 oz) chorizo sausage, cut into 1 cm (½ inch) dice | 2 ripe tomatoes, deseeded and finely chopped | 3 tablespoons chopped flat leaf parsley | 2 x 400 g (13 oz) cans organic chickpeas in water, drained and rinsed | salt and freshly ground black pepper

ONE Heat the oil in a large, nonstick frying pan, add the onion, garlic and chorizo and cook over a medium-high heat, stirring frequently, for 4–5 minutes. **TWO** Add the tomatoes, parsley and chickpeas to the pan and cook, stirring frequently, for 4–5 minutes until heated through. Season to taste with salt and pepper and serve immediately or leave to cool to room temperature.

Serves 4

NUTRIENT ANALYSIS PER SERVING 1737 kJ – 415 kcal – 24 g protein – 36 g carbohydrate – 7 g sugars – 21 g fat – 6 g saturates – 10 g fibre – 300 mg sodium

HEALTHY TIP Chickpeas are a great source of dietary fibre and they also contain iron, which is essential for healthy blood. The vitamin C from the tomatoes in this dish will help in the absorption of the iron.

recipe illustrated on pages 56–57

SPICE- AND HERB- MARINATED OLIVES

Little bowls of olives grace the counter of every tapas bar in Spain. The olives will be black, green or purple, and will usually have been cured or marinated, some with spices or garlic and others with chillies. This is a really quick and easy recipe for adding lots of flavour interest to Spanish olives. They can be stored in the refrigerator for up to 2 days.

INGREDIENTS 2 tablespoons red wine vinegar │ 3 garlic cloves, thinly sliced │ 1 tablespoon coriander seeds │ 2 teaspoons cumin seeds │ 4 tablespoons finely chopped flat leaf parsley │ 1 tablespoon dried red chilli flakes │ 1 teaspoon sweet pimiento │ 500 g (1 lb) mixed green and black olives │ olive oil, for drizzling

ONE Put the vinegar in a small, non-reactive bowl with the garlic, cover with clingfilm and leave the mixture to soak at room temperature for 24 hours. **TWO** Heat a heavy-based frying pan, add the coriander seeds and dry-fry over a medium heat, stirring, until aromatic and lightly browned. Leave to cool, then coarsely crush in a mortar with a pestle. Toast the cumin seeds in the same way, but leave them whole. **THREE** Drain the garlic, discarding the vinegar, and mix in a separate bowl with the parsley, chilli flakes, sweet pimiento, crushed coriander seeds and cumin seeds. **FOUR** Add the olives, drizzle over a little oil and toss to mix well. Cover with clingfilm and leave to marinate at room temperature for 4–5 hours, tossing from time to time, before serving.

Serves 4

NUTRIENT ANALYSIS PER SERVING 540 kJ – 130 kcal – 2 g protein – 2 g carbohydrate – 0 g sugars – 14 g fat – 2 g saturates – 4 g fibre – 2270 mg sodium

HEALTHY TIP Olives are a great source of monounsaturated fats and the antioxidant vitamin E. They are usually preserved by long soaking in brine, which gives them a high sodium content. You can reduce this to some extent by draining the olives and rinsing them thoroughly before marinating.

ANCHOVIES WITH GRILLED RED PEPPERS

Canned red piquillo peppers normally feature in this much-loved tapas dish, but this recipe uses roasted and skinned fresh red peppers, combined with the anchovies, to make a delicious snack. Serve with a glass of chilled fino sherry.

INGREDIENTS 3 red peppers | 100 g (3½ oz) bottle anchovy fillets in salt | 2 garlic cloves, finely chopped | 2 tablespoons finely chopped flat leaf parsley | extra virgin olive oil, to drizzle

ONE Arrange the peppers on a grill rack and cook under a preheated high grill, turning frequently, for 15–20 minutes or until charred all over. Transfer to a polythene bag and leave to stand for 10–12 minutes for the steam to loosen the skins. **TWO** Carefully peel away the skins, then core and deseed the peppers. Cut the flesh into large bite-sized pieces and arrange in a single layer in a shallow serving dish. **THREE** Rinse and dry the anchovy fillets, cut them in half lengthways and arrange them over the peppers in the dish. Scatter over the garlic and parsley, and drizzle a little olive oil over the anchovies before serving.

Serves 4

NUTRIENT ANALYSIS PER SERVING 490 kJ –118 kcal – 8 g protein – 7 g carbohydrate – 6 g sugars – 7 g fat – 0 g saturates – 2 g fibre – 987 mg sodium

HEALTHY TIP Anchovies contain the valuable omega-3 fatty acids thought to be important in the maintenance of levels of 'good' HDL cholesterol. Draining and rinsing the anchovies will remove some of the salt content, but not all, so do not add any extra salt to the dish.

SAUTÉED SWEET GREEN PEPPERS

From the north-westerly provinces of Spain, these small, sweet green peppers come into the market in spring and summer. They make a delicious appetizer and are best eaten with your fingers. But beware – like Russian roulette, one in every ten of these peppers turns out to be fiery hot! Padrón peppers are available from Spanish greengrocers and suppliers.

INGREDIENTS 400 g (13 oz) small sweet green Padrón peppers │ olive oil, for shallow-frying │ sea salt

ONE Rinse the peppers, leaving the stems intact, and pat dry with kitchen paper. **TWO** Drizzle a little oil into a large, nonstick frying pan and heat over a high heat. Add the peppers to the pan and cook over a medium heat, turning frequently, until lightly browned all over. **THREE** Remove the peppers with a slotted spoon and drain on crumpled kitchen paper. Transfer to a serving dish and sprinkle over a little sea salt. Serve immediately.

Serves 4–6

NUTRIENT ANALYSIS PER SERVING 268 kJ – 64 kcal – 1 g protein – 3 g carbohydrate – 2 g sugars – 6 g fat – 1 g saturates – 2 g fibre – 500 mg sodium

HEALTHY TIP Green peppers are a great source of the antioxidant betacarotene, which is believed to protect against cancer, heart disease and stroke.

recipe illustrated on pages 64–65

SPINACH OMELETTE

A firm tapas favourite, this tortilla also makes for a great meal-in-a-hurry. You could use whatever cooked leftover vegetables you have at hand instead of the spinach if you prefer.

INGREDIENTS 200 g (7 oz) baby spinach leaves │ 2 tablespoons olive oil │ 1 small onion, finely chopped │ 250 g (8 oz) potatoes, peeled, cut into 1.5 cm (¾ inch) dice, cooked until just tender and cooled │ 6 large eggs │ salt and freshly ground black pepper

ONE Cook the spinach in a large saucepan of lightly salted boiling water for 1–2 minutes. Drain the spinach thoroughly, squeezing out any excess liquid, then roughly chop. Set aside. **TWO** Heat the oil in a 20 cm (8 inch) nonstick frying pan with a flameproof handle (or cover the handle with foil), add the onion and cook over a low heat, stirring occasionally, for 8–10 minutes until softened. Add the potatoes and cook, stirring, for 2–3 minutes. Add the spinach and stir to mix well. **THREE** Lightly beat the eggs in a bowl and season to taste with salt and pepper. Pour into the pan and cook over a low heat, shaking the pan frequently, for 10–12 minutes until set on the bottom. **FOUR** Put the pan under a preheated medium grill and cook for 2–3 minutes or until the top is set and lightly browned. **FIVE** Remove from the heat and leave to rest for 3–4 minutes before turning out on to a chopping board. Cut into wedges or squares and serve.

Serves 4–6

NUTRIENT ANALYSIS PER SERVING 980 kJ – 235 kcal – 13 g protein – 13 g carbohydrate – 2 g sugars – 15 g fat – 3 g saturates – 3 g fibre – 190 mg sodium

HEALTHY TIP Spinach is a good source of folic acid, the B-group vitamin essential for cell formation. Folic acid can be destroyed by heating, so cook spinach as quickly as possible to preserve its nutritional value.

POTATOES WITH TOMATOES

This classic tapa is a must when partaking of a little glass of chilled fino sherry in a tapas bar. The potatoes are usually fried, but here they have been oven-roasted instead to reduce the amount of fat required.

INGREDIENTS 800 g (1 lb 10 oz) potatoes, peeled, cut into bite-sized pieces and cooked until just tender | olive oil, for drizzling | 400 g (13 oz) can chopped tomatoes | 1 small red onion, finely chopped | 2 garlic cloves, finely chopped | 3 teaspoons pimentón dulce (mild paprika) | 1 bay leaf | 1 teaspoon golden caster sugar | salt | finely chopped flat leaf parsley, to garnish

ONE Line a baking sheet with baking paper. Arrange the potatoes in a single layer on the prepared baking sheet. Drizzle over a little oil and season to taste with salt and pepper. Roast in a preheated oven, 220°C (425°F), Gas Mark 7, for 15–20 minutes until lightly browned. **TWO** Meanwhile, put the tomatoes and their juice, onion and garlic in a saucepan and cook over a medium heat, stirring occasionally, for 10–15 minutes. Add the pimentón, bay leaf and sugar and cook, stirring frequently, for a further 5–10 minutes. **THREE** Transfer the potatoes to a warmed serving dish and pour over the tomato sauce. Toss to mix well and serve, garnished with chopped parsley.

Serves 4

NUTRIENT ANALYSIS PER SERVING 824 kJ – 195 kcal – 6 g protein – 40 g carbohydrate – 6 g sugars – 2 g fat – 0 g saturates – 4 g fibre – 54 mg sodium

HEALTHY TIP To preserve the vitamin C content of the potatoes, peel them as thinly as possible just before cooking. Garlic and onions may both have a role in the prevention of blood clots, and thus in protection against coronary heart disease.

recipe illustrated on pages 70–71

STUFFED TOMATOES

These stuffed tomatoes, flavoured with garlic and herbs, make a great tapa to serve with drinks. You can also use them to accompany any grilled meat, poultry or fish dish.

INGREDIENTS 4 large ripe tomatoes | 2 tablespoons olive oil | 2 tablespoons pine nuts | 3 garlic cloves, finely chopped | 100 g (3½ oz) fresh white breadcrumbs | 1 tablespoon chopped tarragon leaves | 1 tablespoon chopped flat leaf parsley | salt and freshly ground black pepper

ONE Cut the tomatoes in half widthways, then scoop out and discard the seeds. Using a small teaspoon, carefully hollow out the tomato shells, reserving the flesh. Arrange the tomato halves, cut-side up, on a baking sheet. **TWO** Heat the oil in a nonstick frying pan, add the pine nuts and cook over a medium heat, stirring constantly, for 2–3 minutes. Add the garlic, breadcrumbs and herbs and cook, stirring constantly, for 3–4 minutes. Add the reserved tomato flesh, season to taste with salt and pepper and cook, continuing to stir, for 2–3 minutes. **THREE** Spoon an equal quantity of the mixture into each tomato shell and bake in a preheated oven, 180°C (350°F), Gas Mark 4, for 15–20 minutes until the tomatoes have softened. **FOUR** Remove the tomatoes from the oven and leave to cool to room temperature before serving.

Serves 4

NUTRIENT ANALYSIS PER SERVING 755 kJ – 180 kcal – 4 g protein – 18 g carbohydrate – 6 g sugars – 11 g fat – 3 g saturates – 3 g fibre – 144 mg sodium

HEALTHY TIP Tomatoes are an excellent source of vitamin C and betacarotene. Both of these act as antioxidants, removing free radicals that may cause cancers.

MUSSELS WITH VINAIGRETTE

About 90 per cent of the mussels in Spain are harvested off the Galician 'sunshine coast'. Here they are served as a tapa with a simple vinaigrette dressing. Serve with crusty bread.

INGREDIENTS 1 kg (2 lb) live mussels, prepared *(see page 16)* │ 3 garlic cloves, finely chopped │ 200 ml (7 fl oz) fino sherry │ 100 ml (3½ fl oz) cold water

VINAIGRETTE 3 tablespoons olive oil │ 2 tablespoons white wine vinegar │ 1 tablespoon very finely chopped shallot │ 1 tablespoon very finely chopped, drained canned or bottled pimiento │ 1 tablespoon very finely chopped parsley │ salt and freshly ground black pepper

ONE Put the drained mussels in a large, shallow frying pan. Sprinkle over the garlic, sherry and measurement water. Cover tightly and cook over a high heat, shaking the pan vigorously several times, for 4–5 minutes or until all the mussels have opened (discard any that remain closed). **TWO** Meanwhile, to make the vinaigrette, mix all the ingredients together in a small bowl and season to taste with salt and pepper. **THREE** Remove the empty half mussel shells and discard. Arrange the mussels in their half shells in a single layer in a shallow serving dish or use 4 smaller dishes. Spoon the vinaigrette over the mussels and serve immediately.

Serves 4

NUTRIENT ANALYSIS PER SERVING 846 kJ – 200 kcal – 13 g protein – 2 g carbohydrate – 1 g sugars – 10 g fat – 1 g saturates – 0 g fibre – 165 mg sodium

HEALTHY TIP Mussels contain vitamin B12 and folic acid, and are also a source of selenium and zinc. The trace mineral zinc is essential for the healing of body tissue.

recipe illustrated on pages 76–77

EGGS WITH VEGETABLES

This wonderful combination of slowly cooked tomatoes, peppers and aubergines was thought to have been brought to Europe by the Basques from Mexico, home of the pepper. In this recipe, lightly beaten eggs are stirred into the vegetable mixture, but you can also serve it topped with fried or poached eggs.

INGREDIENTS 2 tablespoons olive oil │ 1 onion, very finely chopped │ 4 garlic cloves, thinly sliced │ 2 red peppers, cored, deseeded and thinly sliced │ 200 g (7 oz) aubergine, cut into 1 cm (½ inch) dice │ 400 g (13 oz) can chopped tomatoes │ 1 teaspoon soft light brown sugar │ 4 small eggs │ salt and freshly ground black pepper │ chopped flat leaf parsley, to garnish

ONE Heat the oil in a heavy-based frying pan, add the onion and cook over a low heat, stirring occasionally for 12–15 minutes or until soft and lightly browned. **TWO** Add the garlic, red peppers and aubergine and cook over a medium heat, stirring frequently, for 3–4 minutes. **THREE** Stir in the tomatoes and their juice and sugar, season to taste with salt and pepper and bring to the boil. Reduce the heat, cover and cook over a low heat for 25–30 minutes until the mixture has thickened. **FOUR** Lightly beat the eggs and stir them into the pan. Remove the pan from the heat, cover and leave to stand for 5–6 minutes or until the eggs are just set. **FIVE** Sprinkle over chopped parsley to garnish and serve immediately in little bowls as a tapa or in the pan as a main course.

Serves 4 as a tapa or 2 as a main course

NUTRIENT ANALYSIS PER SERVING 840 kJ – 200 kcal – 10 g protein – 14 g carbohydrate – 13 g sugars – 12 g fat – 3 g saturates – 4 g fibre – 122 mg sodium

HEALTHY TIP Eggs are an excellent source of protein and iron for non-meat eaters. The tomatoes and peppers in the recipe are rich in vitamin C, which helps the absorption of iron.

SOUPS AND

SALADS

GALICIAN-STYLE BROTH

This hearty vegetable and meat soup from Galicia is cooked altogether in one pot. It traditionally uses salt pork belly, but lean smoked bacon has been substituted here for a healthier version.

INGREDIENTS 2.5 litres (4 pints) cold water | 200 g (7 oz) white haricot beans, soaked overnight in cold water and drained | 125 g (4 oz) lean smoked bacon, in one piece | 125 g (4 oz) Serrano ham, in one piece | 200 g (7 oz) stewing beef, in one piece | 2 onions, thickly sliced | 350 g (11½ oz) potatoes, peeled and quartered | 4 small white turnips, peeled and halved | 300 g (10 oz) chopped green cabbage | salt and freshly ground black pepper

ONE Put the measurement water in a large, heavy-based saucepan with the beans, bacon, ham, beef and onions. Bring to the boil, skimming off any foam that rises to the surface. Reduce the heat, cover and cook over a very low heat for about 1½ hours. **TWO** Add the potatoes and turnips, re-cover and cook for 20–25 minutes or until tender. Add the cabbage, re-cover and cook for a further 10 minutes. Season to taste with salt and pepper and remove from the heat. **THREE** Remove the meats with a slotted spoon and cut into bite-sized portions. Ladle the soup into large warmed bowls and top with the meats. Serve immediately.

Serves 4

NUTRIENT ANALYSIS PER SERVING 1873 kJ – 444 kcal – 40 g protein – 50 g carbohydrate – 11 g sugars – 10 g fat – 3 g saturates – 17 g fibre – 1280 mg sodium

HEALTHY TIP The addition of potatoes and haricot beans makes this a highly nutritious one-pot meal, with a balanced combination of proteins and carbohydrate. Avoid adding additional salt, as the ham and bacon mean that the sodium level is already quite high.

15-MINUTE SOUP

This Iberian soup makes use of both fresh and storecupboard ingredients for a fantastically quick yet satisfying afterwork supper. It is ideal followed by a crisp green salad.

INGREDIENTS 2 tablespoons olive oil | 1 small onion, finely chopped | 2 garlic cloves, finely chopped | 2 thick slices of day-old bread, crusts removed, broken into pieces | 2 tomatoes, roughly chopped | 1 litre (1¾ pints) shop-bought or homemade Vegetable Stock *(see page 19)* | 200 g (7 oz) frozen peas | 1 teaspoon pimentón dulce (mild paprika) | 100 ml (3½ fl oz) fino sherry | 250 g (8 oz) raw tiger prawns in their shells | 1 hard-boiled egg, shelled and finely chopped | 2 tablespoons finely chopped flat leaf parsley | salt and freshly ground black pepper

ONE Heat the oil in a medium saucepan, add the onion, garlic and bread and cook over a medium heat, stirring frequently, for 3–4 minutes. **TWO** Add the tomatoes, stock, peas, pimentón and sherry and bring to the boil. Reduce the heat and cook over a medium heat, stirring occasionally, for 3–4 minutes. **THREE** Add the prawns and cook, stirring frequently, for 5–7 minutes or until the prawns turn pink and are just cooked through. Remove from the heat and season to taste with salt and pepper. **FOUR** Ladle into warmed shallow bowls, scatter over the egg and parsley and serve immediately.

Serves 4–6

NUTRIENT ANALYSIS PER SERVING 1000 kJ – 239 kcal – 15 g protein – 20 g carbohydrate – 5 g sugars – 8 g fat – 2 g saturates – 5 g fibre – 240 mg sodium

HEALTHY TIP Consuming onions and garlic may help to prevent blood clotting and heart disease. Onions also contain allicin and sulphoraphane, which have been thought to reduce the risk of some cancers.

recipe illustrated on pages 88–89

CHILLED WHITE ALMOND AND GRAPE SOUP

This pale chilled soup is the perfect starter for a really hot summer's day lunch or dinner. Use the best-quality Spanish almonds you can find for a superior flavour.

INGREDIENTS 4 slices of day-old bread, crusts removed, broken into pieces │ 100 g (3½ oz) whole blanched almonds │ 2 garlic cloves, finely chopped │ 4 tablespoons extra virgin olive oil, plus extra for drizzling │ 4 tablespoons red wine vinegar │ 1 litre (1¾ pints) iced water │ 100 g (3½ oz) peeled seedless white or green grapes, roughly chopped │ salt

ONE Soak the bread in a bowl of cold water for 5–6 minutes. **TWO** Meanwhile, put the almonds in a food processor with the garlic and process in bursts until finely ground. **THREE** Drain the bread and squeeze out the excess liquid. Add to the almond mixture and process until smooth. Add the oil and vinegar and continue to process until smooth. With the machine running, pour in the measurement iced water in a thin stream and process until smooth. **FOUR** Strain the mixture through a fine sieve, pressing down hard to extract as much liquid as you can. Season to taste with salt, cover and chill in the refrigerator for 8–10 hours or overnight. **FIVE** Just before serving, pour the mixture into individual chilled bowls and top each bowl with an equal quantity of the grapes. Drizzle with olive oil and serve immediately.

Serves 4

NUTRIENT ANALYSIS PER SERVING 1470 kJ – 353 kcal – 8 g protein – 21 g carbohydrate – 6 g sugars – 27g fat – 3 g saturates – 2 g fibre – 163 mg sodium

HEALTHY TIP Almonds contain high levels of vitamin E, as well as useful amounts of B vitamins and some minerals. Grapes provide carotene, which the body uses to make vitamin A, as well as small amounts of B vitamins and vitamin C.

ANDALUSIAN GAZPACHO

This classic chilled soup, deliciously refreshing on a hot summer's day, was traditionally made in a Spanish mortar or *mortero*. However, in today's world, a blender or food processor takes all the hard work out of the preparation without compromising the flavour of the original.

INGREDIENTS 1 kg (2 lb) vine-ripened tomatoes | 2 slices of day-old crusty bread | 1 red pepper, cored, deseeded and roughly chopped | 2 garlic cloves, finely chopped | 1 teaspoon golden caster sugar | 2–3 tablespoons red wine vinegar | 2–3 tablespoons extra virgin olive oil | a few drops of Tabasco sauce | salt and freshly ground black pepper
OVEN-BAKED CROUTONS 2 thick slices of bread | olive oil, for brushing
GARNISH TOPPINGS 4 tablespoons finely diced cucumber | 3 tablespoons finely diced red onion | chopped flat leaf parsley

ONE Score a cross in the base of each tomato. Put in a heatproof bowl, pour over boiling water to cover and leave for 10–15 seconds. Drain and plunge into cold water, then peel away the skins. Cut the tomatoes in half. Deseed and roughly chop the flesh, then transfer to a blender or food processor. **TWO** Break the bread into pieces and soak in a bowl of cold water for 5–6 minutes, then drain and squeeze out the excess liquid. Add to the tomatoes in the blender or food processor with the red pepper, garlic, sugar, vinegar, oil and Tabasco. Blend until smooth, adding a little chilled water if you want a thinner consistency. Season to taste with salt and pepper, then transfer to a bowl. Cover and chill in the refrigerator for 3–4 hours. **THREE** Meanwhile, to make the croûtons, remove the crusts from the bread and cut the bread into cubes. Lightly brush a baking sheet with oil. Spread the bread cubes out on the baking sheet and brush lightly with oil. Bake in a preheated oven, 200°C (400°F), Gas Mark 6, for 10–15 minutes until golden and crisp. Transfer to a wire rack and leave to cool. **FOUR** To serve, ladle the gazpacho into chilled bowls and top with a little of each of the garnish toppings and the croûtons. Serve the remainder in small bowls for people to help themselves.

Serves 4–6

NUTRIENT ANALYSIS PER SERVING 1070 kJ – 254 kcal – 7 g protein – 36 g carbohydrate – 12 g sugars – 10 g fat – 2 g saturates – 6 g fibre – 286 mg sodium

HEALTHY TIP Tomatoes and peppers are brilliant sources of vitamin C and betacarotenes, both very important for their antioxidant properties. Tomatoes also contain lycopene, a pigment that produces the tomato's red colour and which may help to protect against bladder and pancreatic cancers.

recipe illustrated on pages 94–95

CHICKEN SOUP WITH LEMON AND MINT

Popular in both Spain and Portugal, this clear chicken soup, which has been flavoured with fresh mint and lemon, is comfort food at its best.

INGREDIENTS 1 small whole chicken, about 1 kg (2 lb), jointed | 2 litres (3½ pints) water or shop-bought or homemade Vegetable Stock *(see page 19)* | 2 onions, finely chopped | 1 bay leaf | 3 tablespoons paella rice, such as Calasparra or Bomba, or other short-grain rice | 2 tablespoons lemon juice | 8 tablespoons finely chopped fresh mint leaves | salt and freshly ground black pepper

ONE Put the chicken in a large, flameproof casserole with the measurement water or stock, onions and bay leaf and bring to the boil. Reduce the heat, cover tightly and cook over a very low heat for 30 minutes. **TWO** Stir in the rice, re-cover and cook for a further hour. Remove from the heat and leave the chicken to cool in the stock. **THREE** Remove the chicken from the stock with a slotted spoon. Remove and discard the skin and bones. Tear the flesh into bite-sized pieces and return to the casserole. Stir in the lemon juice and reheat the soup until hot. Season to taste with salt and pepper. **FOUR** Add the mint and stir well. Ladle into warmed bowls and serve immediately.

Serves 4

NUTRIENT ANALYSIS PER SERVING 1787 kJ – 430 kcal – 32 g protein – 17 g carbohydrate – 4 g sugars – 26 g fat – 8 g saturates – 1 g fibre – 129 mg sodium

HEALTHY TIP When the chicken and stock have cooled, skim as much fat from the surface as you can. Alternatively, remove the skin from the chicken before starting the cooking process.

SALAD OF SALT COD WITH TOMATOES AND PEPPERS

Salt cod is highly esteemed in Spanish cooking and here it is accompanied by ripe tomatoes and peppers to make a robust and colourful salad that is substantial enough to serve as a main course.

INGREDIENTS 400 g (13 oz) salt cod | 2 red peppers, cored, deseeded and thinly sliced | 4 ripe tomatoes, thinly sliced | juice of 1 lemon | extra virgin olive oil, for drizzling | freshly ground black pepper | chopped flat leaf parsley, to garnish

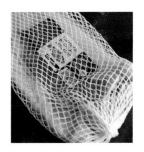

ONE Soak the cod in a bowl of cold water overnight, changing the water 3–4 times to remove the excess salt. **TWO** Drain, put in a large saucepan, cover with fresh cold water and bring to the boil. Reduce the heat and simmer over a low heat for 15–20 minutes or until tender. **THREE** Drain the fish, remove and discard the skin and bones and coarsely flake the flesh. Transfer to a shallow salad bowl. **FOUR** Mix the red peppers and tomatoes together and add to the fish. Toss to mix well. **FIVE** Pour over the lemon juice and drizzle a little oil over the salad. Season to taste with pepper and sprinkle with chopped parsley before serving.

Serves 4

NUTRIENT ANALYSIS PER SERVING 790 kJ – 186 kcal – 34 g protein – 7 g carbohydrate – 7 g sugars – 3 g fat – 1 g saturates – 2 g fibre – 410 mg sodium

HEALTHY TIP Salt cod is low in fat. It is complemented in this recipe by the addition of peppers and tomatoes, both high in antioxidants. These are thought to prevent cancers by removing the possibly carcinogenic free radicals found naturally in some foods and created through the cooking process in others.

recipe illustrated on pages 100–101

RICE AND OLIVE SALAD

INGREDIENTS 400 g (13 oz) cold cooked long-grain white rice │ 4 spring onions, finely chopped │ 1 garlic clove, very finely chopped │ 1 red pepper, cored, deseeded and very finely chopped │ 15 black olives, pitted and finely chopped │ 15 green olives, pitted and finely chopped │ 12 cherry tomatoes, halved │ 4 tablespoons chopped flat leaf parsley │ juice of 1 lemon │ 2 tablespoons olive oil │ salt and freshly ground black pepper

ONE Put the rice in a shallow salad bowl and fluff up the grains with a fork to separate. **TWO** Add the spring onions, garlic, red pepper, olives, tomatoes and parsley and stir to mix well. **THREE** Pour over the lemon juice and drizzle over the oil. Season to taste with salt and pepper and toss to mix well. Serve immediately.

Serves 4

NUTRIENT ANALYSIS PER SERVING 1000 kJ – 239 kcal – 4 g protein – 35 g carbohydrate – 5 g sugars – 10 g fat – 2 g saturates – 4 g fibre – 855 mg sodium

HEALTHY TIP Olives are rich in monounsaturated fat, which can help to maintain a higher ratio of 'good' HDL cholesterol to 'bad' LDL cholesterol and so possibly avert cardiovascular disease. To reduce the salt content of olives preserved in brine, rinse well and drain.

GRILLED RED PEPPER SALAD

INGREDIENTS 4 red peppers

DRESSING 1 garlic clove, crushed | 3 tablespoons red wine vinegar | 4 tablespoons olive oil | salt and freshly ground black pepper

ONE Arrange the peppers on a grill rack and cook under a preheated high grill, turning frequently, for 15–20 minutes or until charred all over. Transfer to a polythene bag and leave to stand for 10–12 minutes for the steam to loosen the skins. **TWO** Carefully peel away the skins, then core and deseed the peppers. Cut the flesh into strips and arrange in a shallow bowl in a single layer. **THREE** To make the dressing, mix all the ingredients together in a jug or small bowl, season to taste with salt and pepper and pour over the peppers. Cover and leave to stand at room temperature for 10–15 minutes to allow the flavours to develop before serving.

Serves 4

NUTRIENT ANALYSIS PER SERVING 597 kJ – 144 kcal – 2 g protein – 9 g carbohydrate – 9 g sugars – 12 g fat – 2 g saturates – 3 g fibre – 8 mg sodium

HEALTHY TIP Red peppers are a particularly good source of vitamin C. This vitamin is essential for the maintenance and repair of body tissue, and it is also invaluable for its antioxidant properties.

PEACH AND LETTUCE SALAD

INGREDIENTS 500 g (1 lb) ripe peaches | 4 Little Gem lettuces | 200 ml (7 fl oz) low-fat fromage frais | 100 ml (3½ fl oz) reduced-fat mayonnaise | 2 tablespoons chopped almonds, toasted | salt and freshly ground black pepper

ONE Bring a large saucepan of water to the boil. Add the peaches and leave for 30 seconds. Drain and plunge into cold water, then peel away the skins. **TWO** Cut each peach in half, remove and discard the stones and cut each half into 4 wedges. **THREE** Separate the leaves of the lettuces and arrange around the edge of a salad platter, then put the peach slices in the centre of the dish. **FOUR** Beat the fromage frais and mayonnaise together in a small bowl, season to taste with salt and pepper and spoon over the salad. Sprinkle with the almonds just before serving.

Serves 4

NUTRIENT ANALYSIS PER SERVING 830 kJ – 198 kcal – 8 g protein – 16 g carbohydrate – 15 g sugars – 12 g fat – 1 g saturates – 5 g fibre – 257 mg sodium

HEALTHY TIP Folic acid is found in varying quantities in most vegetables (particularly leafy green ones) and some fruit. Lettuce, especially the greener outer leaves, is an excellent source. Folic acid is essential for the development and maintenance of body cells.

ANDALUSIAN-STYLE SALAD

Typical of this region's approach to hot-weather dining, this wonderfully colourful and refreshing salad makes a great start to a summer meal.

INGREDIENTS 4 ripe tomatoes, sliced or quartered │ 1 red onion, halved and very thinly sliced │ 2 red peppers, cored, deseeded and thinly sliced │ 16 green olives, pitted │ 4 tablespoons olive oil │ 3 tablespoons sherry vinegar │ 1 teaspoon clear honey │ 1 garlic clove, crushed │ salt and freshly ground black pepper │ finely chopped flat leaf parsley, to garnish

ONE Put the tomatoes, onion, red peppers and olives in a shallow salad bowl or on a salad platter. **TWO** Mix the oil, vinegar, honey and garlic together in a jug or small bowl. Season to taste with salt and pepper and pour over the salad. Toss to mix well. **THREE** Cover and leave to stand at room temperature for 15–20 minutes to allow the flavours to develop, then serve, garnished with chopped parsley.

Serves 4

NUTRIENT ANALYSIS PER SERVING 772 kJ – 186 kcal – 2 g protein – 14 g carbohydrate – 13 g sugars – 14 g fat – 2 g saturates – 4 g fibre – 440 mg sodium

HEALTHY TIP Red peppers are a very rich source of carotene, which the body converts to vitamin A. They are also very high in vitamin C, making this salad an extremely good source of antioxidants, thought to be important in the prevention of cancers.

RED ONION AND ORANGE SALAD

INGREDIENTS 4 tablespoons sultanas | 4 large sweet oranges | 1 small red onion, thinly sliced | 20 black olives, pitted | 2 tablespoons flaked almonds | a small handful of mint leaves | 2 tablespoons red wine vinegar | 4 tablespoons olive oil | salt and freshly ground black pepper

ONE Soak the sultanas in a bowl of hot water for 20 minutes to plump up. Drain and transfer to a shallow salad bowl or salad platter. **TWO** Remove the skin and pith from the oranges. Working over a bowl to catch the juice, cut between the membranes to remove the segments. **THREE** Add the orange segments to the bowl or platter with the onion, olives, almonds and mint and toss to mix well. **FOUR** Mix the vinegar and oil together in a jug or small bowl with the reserved orange juice and season to taste with salt and pepper. Pour over the salad and toss to coat evenly. Cover and chill in the refrigerator for 1–2 hours before serving.

Serves 4

NUTRIENT ANALYSIS PER SERVING 1375 kJ – 328 kcal – 5 g protein – 40 g carbohydrate – 40 g sugars – 17 g fat – 2 g saturates – 8 g fibre – 385 mg sodium

HEALTHY TIP This is a very nutritious salad. Oranges have a high vitamin C content and are also a good source of folic acid. Almonds are a good source of vitamin E, and both almonds and raisins contain useful amounts of iron.

POTATO AND VEGETABLE SALAD

This salad is served throughout Spain with little variation. It is a perfectly balanced mixture of potatoes, eggs and vegetables, lightly dressed with mayonnaise to accent the different flavours.

INGREDIENTS 400 g (13 oz) potatoes, peeled and cut into 1.5 cm (¾ inch) dice | 1 large carrot, cut into 1.5 cm (¾ inch) dice | 100 g (3½ oz) fresh or frozen peas | 100 g (3½ oz) green beans, trimmed and cut into 1.5 cm (¾ inch) lengths | ½ onion, finely chopped | 1 small red pepper, cored, deseeded and very finely chopped | 2 tablespoons finely chopped gherkins | 1 tablespoon small capers | 12 red pepper-stuffed green olives | chopped flat leaf parsley, to garnish

DRESSING 150 ml (¼ pint) low-fat mayonnaise | 1 tablespoon lemon juice | 1 teaspoon Dijon mustard | salt and freshly ground black pepper

ONE Bring a large saucepan of lightly salted water to the boil, add the potatoes and carrots and cook for 10–12 minutes or until almost tender. Add the peas and beans and cook for 1–2 minutes. **TWO** Drain the vegetables and transfer to a shallow salad bowl with the onion, red pepper, gherkins, capers and olives. **THREE** Beat all the dressing ingredients together in a small bowl and season to taste with salt and pepper. Spoon over the salad and toss to coat evenly (you may need to do this with your fingers). **FOUR** Garnish with chopped parsley before serving.

Serves 4

NUTRIENT ANALYSIS PER SERVING 988 kJ – 236 kcal – 5 g protein – 27 g carbohydrate – 9 g sugars – 13 g fat – 0 g saturates – 6 g fibre – 796 mg sodium

HEALTHY TIP Most of the vitamin C in potatoes is near the surface of the skin, so peel them as thinly as possible. Vitamin loss will also be reduced if you use a sharp knife.

recipe illustrated on pages 112–113

LEEK SALAD

This attractive salad comes from the Basque region. Try to use baby leeks that are as fresh as possible to add sweetness to the dish.

INGREDIENTS 20–24 baby leeks, trimmed, halved lengthways and cleaned | 4 tablespoons olive oil | 2 tablespoons red wine vinegar | 1 garlic clove, crushed | 1 teaspoon pimentón dulce (mild paprika) | 2 hard-boiled eggs, shelled and finely chopped | salt and freshly ground black pepper

ONE Bring a large saucepan of lightly salted water to the boil, add the leeks and cook for 8–10 minutes or until tender. Drain thoroughly and arrange in a shallow salad bowl. **TWO** Mix the oil, vinegar, garlic and pimentón together in a jug or small bowl. Season to taste with salt and pepper and pour over the leeks. Scatter over the hard-boiled eggs and serve immediately.

Serves 4

NUTRIENT ANALYSIS PER SERVING 740 kJ – 179 kcal – 6 g protein – 5 g carbohydrate – 3 g sugars – 15 g fat – 3 g saturates – 4 g fibre – 46 mg sodium

HEALTHY TIP Leeks are quite high in carotene (used by the body to make vitamin A) and also contain folic acid, particularly in the dark green parts of the vegetable. Folic acid is heat-sensitive, so try to cook green vegetables for as short a time as possible.

VEGETABLES

FENNEL GRATIN

INGREDIENTS 400 g (13 oz) baby fennel or 2 fennel bulbs │ 100 g (3½ oz) fresh curd cheese or ricotta │ 1 tablespoon chopped oregano leaves, plus extra whole leaves to garnish │ olive oil, for drizzling │ salt and freshly ground black pepper

ONE Trim and halve the baby fennel or thickly slice the fennel bulbs. Bring a large saucepan of lightly salted water to the boil, add the fennel and cook for 15–20 minutes. Drain and arrange in a shallow gratin dish in a single layer. **TWO** Crumble over the cheese and scatter over the oregano. Season to taste with salt and pepper and drizzle with a little oil. Cook under a preheated medium-high grill for 6–8 minutes or until lightly golden. Serve immediately, garnished with whole oregano leaves.

Serves 4

NUTRIENT ANALYSIS PER SERVING 259 kJ – 62 kcal – 3 g protein – 2 g carbohydrate – 2 g sugars – 5 g fat – 2 g saturates – 2 g fibre – 36 mg sodium

HEALTHY TIP Although folic acid is usually found in leafy dark green vegetables, fennel – a pale-coloured bulb – contains significant amounts of this B-group vitamin. Folic acid helps ward off anaemia and it is vital for cell formation, especially during the earliest stages of life.

GARLICKY CAULIFLOWER

INGREDIENTS 800 g (1 lb 10 oz) cauliflower florets | 4 tablespoons olive oil | 3 garlic cloves, finely chopped | 1 tablespoon pimentón dulce (mild paprika) | 2 tablespoons white wine vinegar | salt and freshly ground black pepper | finely chopped flat leaf parsley, to garnish

ONE Bring a large saucepan of lightly salted water to the boil. Break the cauliflower florets into bite-sized pieces, add to the pan and cook for 6–8 minutes. Drain thoroughly and set aside. **TWO** Heat the oil in a large, nonstick frying pan. Add the garlic and cook over a medium heat, stirring, for 1–2 minutes. Add the cauliflower, pimentón and vinegar and season to taste with salt and pepper. Cook over a high heat, stirring, for 3–4 minutes, then remove from the heat. Sprinkle over some chopped flat leaf parsley to garnish and serve immediately.

Serves 4

NUTRIENT ANALYSIS PER SERVING 716 kJ – 173 kcal – 8 g protein – 7 g carbohydrate – 5 g sugars – 13 g fat – 2 g saturates – 4 g fibre – 20 mg sodium

HEALTHY TIP Cauliflower provides folic acid and vitamin C, while garlic is thought to have a role in the prevention of blood clots and thus in protection from heart disease.

SPANISH-STYLE GREEN BEANS

INGREDIENTS 1 tablespoon white wine vinegar | 400 g (13 oz) green beans, trimmed | 2 tablespoons olive oil | 1 small onion, finely chopped | 2 garlic cloves, finely chopped | salt and freshly ground black pepper

ONE Bring a saucepan of water to the boil, add the vinegar and beans and cook for 3–4 minutes. Drain, refresh the beans under cold running water and drain again. Pat the beans dry with kitchen paper. **TWO** Heat the oil in a large, nonstick frying pan, add the onion and beans and cook over a medium heat, stirring frequently, for 3–4 minutes. Add the garlic and cook, stirring, for a further minute. **THREE** Season to taste with salt and pepper, then reduce the heat, cover and cook the beans over a very low heat for 5–6 minutes. Serve immediately.

Serves 4

NUTRIENT ANALYSIS PER SERVING 330 kJ – 80 kcal – 2 g protein – 5 g carbohydrate – 3 g sugars – 6 g fat – 1 g saturates – 8 g fibre – 1 mg sodium

HEALTHY TIP Try substituting mangetout for the green beans, to vary the dish. Green beans and mangetout peas both contain good amounts of carotene, which in the body becomes vitamin A, an important antioxidant. Both vegetables are also sources of dietary fibre.

SPRING VEGETABLE STEW

Spring vegetables are used in this recipe from the Basque region to make a delectable, pretty and very tasty one-pot vegetable meal.

INGREDIENTS 2 tablespoons olive oil │ 100 g (3½ oz) baby onions or small shallots, peeled but left whole │ 2 garlic cloves, finely chopped │ 250 g (8 oz) baby new potatoes, peeled and cooked until just tender │ 250 g (8 oz) baby carrots, trimmed and halved or quartered if large │ 250 g (8 oz) shelled fresh or frozen broad beans │ 2 tablespoons half-fat crème fraîche │ salt and freshly ground black pepper │ spring onions, sliced, to garnish

ONE Heat the oil in a large frying pan. Add the baby onions or shallots and garlic, cover and cook over a low heat, stirring occasionally, for 10–12 minutes until the onions or shallots are soft. Add the potatoes and cook over a medium-low heat, stirring frequently, for 3–4 minutes. Remove from the heat, cover and keep warm. **TWO** Bring a saucepan of lightly salted water to the boil, add the carrots and cook for 6–8 minutes or until just tender. Add the broad beans and cook for 2–3 minutes. Drain and transfer to the onion or shallot and potato mixture. **THREE** Add the crème fraîche, season to taste with salt and pepper and toss to combine. Return to the heat and cook over a high heat, stirring, for 2–3 minutes. Serve immediately, garnished with the sliced spring onions.

Serves 4

NUTRIENT ANALYSIS PER SERVING 753 kJ – 180 kcal – 6 g protein – 20 g carbohydrate – 7 g sugars – 9 g fat – 2 g saturates – 3 g fibre – 46 mg sodium

HEALTHY TIP To preserve the vitamin content of all the vegetables in this recipe, try to prepare them as close to cooking time as possible.

recipe illustrated on pages 126–127

CATALAN-STYLE SPINACH

INGREDIENTS 50 g (2 oz) sultanas | 800 g (1 lb 10 oz) spinach, roughly chopped | 2 tablespoons olive oil | 2 garlic cloves, finely chopped | 1 onion, finely chopped | 4 tablespoons pine nuts, lightly toasted | salt and freshly ground black pepper

ONE Soak the sultanas in a bowl of hot water for 20 minutes to plump up. Drain and set aside. **TWO** Bring a large saucepan of water to the boil, add the spinach and cook for 2–3 minutes. Drain and squeeze out the excess liquid. **THREE** Heat the oil in a large, nonstick frying pan, add the garlic and onion and cook over a medium heat, stirring, for 4–5 minutes. **FOUR** Add the drained spinach, sultanas and pine nuts to the pan, season to taste with salt and pepper and cook, stirring, for 2–3 minutes or until warmed through. Serve immediately.

Serves 4

NUTRIENT ANALYSIS PER SERVING 868 kJ – 209 kcal – 8 g protein – 14 g carbohydrate – 13 g sugars – 14 g fat – 1 g saturates – 9 g fibre – 283 mg sodium

HEALTHY TIP Spinach is a helpful source of folic acid (which tends to occur in dark green leafy vegetables). Pine nuts are rich in the antioxidant vitamin E, while sultanas contain the energy-boosting minerals iron and potassium.

BROAD BEANS WITH HAM

INGREDIENTS 800 g (1 lb 10 oz) fresh broad beans in their pods │ 2–3 tablespoons olive oil │ 2 garlic cloves, thinly sliced │ 1 small onion, finely chopped │ 4 tablespoons finely chopped Serrano ham │ 200 ml (7 fl oz) fino sherry │ 200 ml (7 fl oz) water │ 1 teaspoon finely chopped marjoram leaves │ 2 hard-boiled eggs, shelled and finely chopped │ salt and freshly ground black pepper

ONE Remove the beans from their pods. Heat the oil in a large, heavy-based saucepan, add the garlic, onion and ham and cook, stirring, for 3–4 minutes. Add the beans, sherry, measurement water and marjoram, season to taste with salt and pepper and bring to the boil. Reduce the heat to low, cover and simmer gently for 1 hour or until the beans are tender. **TWO** Uncover the pan and cook to evaporate the remaining liquid (the mixture should be moist, but not too liquid). **THREE** Transfer to a warmed serving dish and scatter over the eggs. Serve immediately.

Serves 4

NUTRIENT ANALYSIS PER SERVING 1090 kJ – 260 kcal – 14 g protein – 9 g carbohydrate – 3 g sugars – 13 g fat – 3 g saturates – 4 g fibre – 348 mg sodium

HEALTHY TIP Broad beans are a great source of dietary fibre and contain quite high levels of carotene, the vitamin A precursor.

AROMATIC DRESSED ARTICHOKES

If you are unable to find fresh artichokes for this dish, use top-quality bottled or canned artichoke hearts, drain well and pat dry with kitchen paper before pouring over the spiced dressing.

INGREDIENTS 4 globe artichokes │ 2 garlic cloves, crushed │ 1 teaspoon ground cumin │ 1 teaspoon ground coriander │ ½ teaspoon dried red chilli flakes │ 1 tablespoon finely chopped oregano leaves │ 2 tablespoons sherry vinegar │ 2 tablespoons shop-bought or homemade Vegetable Stock *(see page 19)* │ 4 tablespoons olive oil │ salt and freshly ground black pepper │ finely chopped flat leaf parsley, to garnish

ONE Trim the artichokes, cutting off the stalks to within 5 cm (2 inches) of the base, and remove and discard the tough outer leaves. Cut off the top quarter of the leaves from each artichoke and cut each one lengthways in half or in quarters if large. **TWO** Using a teaspoon, scoop out and discard the hairy 'choke' from the centre of the artichoke sections and put in a bowl of water with a little lemon juice added to prevent discoloration. **THREE** Bring a large saucepan of lightly salted water to the boil, add the artichokes and return to the boil. Reduce the heat and simmer gently for 20–25 minutes or until tender. Remove with a slotted spoon, drain, cut-side down, on kitchen paper and leave to cool. **FOUR** Meanwhile, to make the dressing, mix the garlic, cumin, coriander, chilli flakes, oregano, vinegar, stock and oil together in a bowl until well combined and season to taste with salt and pepper. **FIVE** Arrange the artichokes in a shallow serving dish in a single layer. Pour over the dressing, cover and leave to stand at room temperature for 15–20 minutes before serving, garnished with chopped parsley.

Serves 4 as a tapa

NUTRIENT ANALYSIS PER SERVING 466 kJ – 113 kcal – 2 g protein – 2 g carbohydrate – 1 g sugars – 11 g fat – 2 g saturates – 1 g fibre – 16 mg sodium

HEALTHY TIP Artichokes are a good source of some minerals and trace minerals, including phosphorus, magnesium, manganese and chromium. They also contain cynarin and sylmarin, which are thought to help the liver regenerate healthy tissue.

recipe illustrated on pages 134–135

CHICKPEAS WITH SWISS CHARD

The nutritious chickpea is a highly versatile pulse and it is also very inexpensive. Here it is teamed with tender Swiss chard, but you can use any other leafy greens instead in this recipe. If you are short of time, use a 400 g (13 oz) can of chickpeas instead of preparing chickpeas from dried.

INGREDIENTS 250 g (8 oz) dried chickpeas | 750 ml (1¼ pints) water | 1 large carrot, cut into small dice | 1 flat leaf parsley sprig | 1 bay leaf | 1 large onion, chopped | 2 tablespoons olive oil | 2 garlic cloves, chopped | 1 red onion, finely chopped | 2 ripe tomatoes, roughly chopped | 250 g (8 oz) Swiss chard, roughly chopped | salt and freshly ground black pepper

ROASTED VEGETABLE SALAD

In this Catalan dish, a colourful selection of classic Mediterranean vegetables are roasted in the oven and then tossed with a cumin- and rosemary-flavoured dressing. Serve with crusty bread.

INGREDIENTS 2 onions, cut into thick wedges | 1 aubergine, cut into thick slices | 1 red pepper, cored, deseeded and thickly sliced | 1 yellow pepper, cored, deseeded and thickly sliced | 2 tomatoes, cut into thick wedges | 8 garlic cloves in their skins | olive oil, for drizzling | salt and freshly ground pepper

DRESSING 2 teaspoons cumin seeds | 2 tablespoons lemon juice | 3 tablespoons sherry vinegar | 4 tablespoons olive oil | 1 teaspoon pimentón dulce (mild paprika) | 1 teaspoon finely chopped rosemary leaves

ONE Spread all the vegetables and garlic out over 2 baking sheets and lightly drizzle with oil. Roast in a preheated oven, 190°C (375°F), Gas Mark 5, for 25–30 minutes. **TWO** Remove from the oven and, when cool enough to handle, slip the garlic cloves from their skins into a blender or food processor. Add all the dressing ingredients and blend until smooth. **THREE** Arrange the vegetables in a serving dish and pour over the dressing. Toss to mix well, season to taste with salt and pepper and serve warm or at room temperature.

Serves 4

NUTRIENT ANALYSIS PER SERVING 812 kJ – 195 kcal – 4 g protein – 16 g carbohydrate – 13 g sugars – 14 g fat – 2 g saturates – 6 g fibre – 17 mg sodium

HEALTHY TIP Onions and garlic are both thought to help prevent blood clots and preserve a healthy heart. Red and yellow peppers are high in vitamin C and carotene and so have powerful antioxidant properties.

CHICKPEAS WITH SWISS CHARD

The nutritious chickpea is a highly versatile pulse and it is also very inexpensive. Here it is teamed with tender Swiss chard, but you can use any other leafy greens instead in this recipe. If you are short of time, use a 400 g (13 oz) can of chickpeas instead of preparing chickpeas from dried.

INGREDIENTS 250 g (8 oz) dried chickpeas | 750 ml (1¼ pints) water | 1 large carrot, cut into small dice | 1 flat leaf parsley sprig | 1 bay leaf | 1 large onion, chopped | 2 tablespoons olive oil | 2 garlic cloves, chopped | 1 red onion, finely chopped | 2 ripe tomatoes, roughly chopped | 250 g (8 oz) Swiss chard, roughly chopped | salt and freshly ground black pepper

ONE Soak the chickpeas in plenty of cold water overnight. Drain, rinse and put in a large saucepan with the measurement water, carrot, parsley sprig, bay leaf and onion. Bring to the boil, skimming off any foam that rises to the surface, then reduce the heat and simmer, uncovered, for 20–25 minutes or until tender. **TWO** Meanwhile, heat the oil in a frying pan, add the garlic and red onion and cook over a medium heat, stirring, for 3–4 minutes. Increase the heat, add the tomatoes and cook, stirring frequently, for 5–6 minutes. **THREE** Add the tomato mixture to the pan of chickpeas and stir in the Swiss chard. Only season to taste with salt and pepper now (the chickpeas will not soften if salt is added before they are tender) and bring to the boil. Reduce the heat and simmer gently, uncovered, for 5–6 minutes. Transfer to a warmed serving bowl.

Serves 4

NUTRIENT ANALYSIS PER SERVING 1344 kJ – 319 kcal – 16 g protein – 45 g carbohydrate – 12 g sugars – 10 g fat – 1 g saturates – 12 g fibre – 170 mg sodium

HEALTHY TIP Chickpeas are highly nutritious, providing useful amounts of protein, carbohydrate, iron and fibre. Swiss chard contains some carotene, vitamin C and folic acid, in addition to small quantities of the B vitamins and trace minerals.

recipe illustrated on pages 140–141

GRIDDLED ASPARAGUS WITH LEMON MAYONNAISE

This Andalusian recipe is a wonderfully simple treatment of a delicate vegetable. If you can, try to find wild asparagus in the spring. This recipe uses a reduced-fat mayonnaise, flavoured with lemon, to accompany the green beauties in healthy style.

INGREDIENTS 800 g (1 lb 10 oz) asparagus spears, trimmed and bases peeled | 3 tablespoons olive oil | salt and freshly ground black pepper

LEMON MAYONNAISE 200 ml (7 fl oz) reduced-fat mayonnaise | 2 garlic cloves, crushed | 2 teaspoons finely grated lemon rind | 2 tablespoons lemon juice | pinch of pimentón dulce (mild paprika)

ONE Arrange the asparagus in a shallow dish in a single layer. Drizzle over the oil and season to taste with salt and pepper. Gently turn the asparagus to coat evenly with the oil.

TWO To make the lemon mayonnaise, beat all the ingredients together in a small bowl and season to taste with salt and pepper. Cover and set aside. **THREE** Heat a large, heavy-based griddle pan over a high heat until smoking. Add the asparagus, in batches, and cook for 2–3 minutes on each side or until lightly charred at the edges. Remove from the pan and keep hot while cooking the remaining asparagus. Serve hot with the lemon mayonnaise.

Serves 4

NUTRIENT ANALYSIS PER SERVING 1107 kJ – 268 kcal – 6 g protein – 8 g carbohydrate – 6 g sugars – 24 g fat – 1 g saturates – 3 g fibre – 470 mg sodium

HEALTHY TIP Asparagus is a good source of folic acid and of the vitamin A precursor, carotene. Cook the asparagus for as short a time as possible to minimize loss of folic acid in cooking.

recipe illustrated on pages 144–145

SAUTÉED MUSHROOMS WITH PARSLEY AND GARLIC

INGREDIENTS 500 g (1 lb) large mushrooms, trimmed │ 4 tablespoons olive oil │ 3 garlic cloves, finely chopped │ 4 tablespoons finely chopped flat leaf parsley │ 3 tablespoons fresh white breadcrumbs │ salt and freshly ground black pepper

ONE Cut the mushrooms in half or quarters, or thinly slice them. Heat the oil in a large frying pan, add the mushrooms, garlic and parsley and cook over a medium heat, stirring frequently, for 6–8 minutes or until the mushrooms are lightly browned and have released all their liquid. **TWO** Stir in the breadcrumbs, season to taste with salt and pepper and stir to mix. Serve immediately.

Serves 4

NUTRIENT ANALYSIS PER SERVING 615 kJ – 148 kcal – 4 g protein – 7 g carbohydrate – 1 g sugars – 12 g fat – 2 g saturates – 4 g fibre – 73 mg sodium

HEALTHY TIP Mushrooms provide potassium, which regulates blood pressure and helps the body beat fatigue. Some types of mushroom are considered capable of warding off viruses and combating allergies.

SPINACH, TOMATO AND PINE NUT FLATBREAD

INGREDIENTS 150 g (5 oz) strong white bread flour, plus extra for dusting │ 8 g (scant ¼ oz) sachet of fast-action dried yeast │ 1 tablespoon very finely chopped rosemary │ 1 teaspoon sea salt │ 2 teaspoons olive oil, plus extra for oiling and drizzling │ 125 ml (4 fl oz) hand-hot water │ freshly ground black pepper

TOPPING 100 g (3½ oz) baby spinach leaves, roughly chopped │ 1 small onion, halved and very thinly sliced │ 2 garlic cloves, thinly sliced │ 200 g (7 oz) small cherry tomatoes │ 1 tablespoon pine nuts

ONE Put the flour in a bowl with the yeast, rosemary and salt. Season to taste with pepper. Make a well in the centre and pour in the oil and the measurement hand-hot water. Using your fingers, mix the wet ingredients into the dry until a dough forms and comes away from the side of the bowl, adding a little extra water if the mixture seems too dry. **TWO** Transfer the dough to a lightly floured work surface and knead for 6–8 minutes. Form the dough into a ball. Put the dough in a lightly oiled bowl, cover and set aside in a warm place for 1 hour or until almost doubled in size. **THREE** Turn out the dough on to a floured work surface and flatten. Roll out with a rolling pin to a rectangle about 25 x 20 cm (10 x 8 inches) and 1 cm (½ inch) thick. Transfer to a nonstick baking sheet. **FOUR** Spread the dough with the spinach and scatter over the onion, garlic and tomatoes. Drizzle over a little oil, season to taste with salt and pepper and scatter over the pine nuts. **FIVE** Bake in a preheated oven, 220°C (425°F), Gas Mark 7, for 12–15 minutes or until the bread is slightly risen and golden. Cut into rectangles and serve warm or at room temperature.

Serves 4

NUTRIENT ANALYSIS PER SERVING 765 kJ – 180 kcal – 6 g protein – 32 g carbohydrate – 3 g sugars – 4 g fat – 1 g saturates – 4 g fibre – 534 mg sodium

HEALTHY TIP Cherry tomatoes are a great source of vitamin C and carotene, and they also have a higher fibre content than larger tomatoes, because of the increased ratio of skin to flesh.

MEAT AND

POULTRY

QUAILS WITH PINE NUTS AND SULTANAS

INGREDIENTS 50 g (2 oz) sultanas | 2 quails, 150–200 g (5–7 oz) each | 3 tablespoons olive oil | 25 g (1 oz) pine nuts | 50 ml (2 fl oz) fino sherry | salt and freshly ground black pepper

ONE Soak the sultanas in a bowl of hot water for about 1 hour to plump up. **TWO** Meanwhile, arrange the quails on a baking sheet and rub 2 tablespoons of the oil all over them. Season to taste with salt and pepper and roast in a preheated oven, 190°C (375°F), Gas Mark 5, for 15–20 minutes or until cooked through, tender and golden. Remove from the oven and transfer to a warmed serving dish. Cover with foil and leave to rest in a warm place while you finish preparing the dish. **THREE** Heat the remaining oil in a small frying pan. Drain the sultanas, add to the pan with the pine nuts and cook, stirring, for 2–3 minutes. Add the sherry and cook, stirring, for 1 minute. Spoon the mixture over the quails and serve immediately.

Serves 2

NUTRIENT ANALYSIS PER SERVING 2044 kJ – 490 kcal – 30 g protein – 18 g carbohydrate – 18 g sugars – 31 g fat – 4 g saturates – 2 g fibre – 80 mg sodium

HEALTHY TIP Like most nuts, pine nuts are a good source of the antioxidant vitamin E. There is some evidence that vitamin E may be protective against heart disease and cancers.

CHICKEN AND CHICKPEA STEW

A *cocido* is the Spanish name for a one-pot dish that is always based on pulses. This hearty chickpea and chicken example originates from Madrid and is usually eaten as a midday meal.

INGREDIENTS 350 g (11½ oz) dried chickpeas | 1.5 kg (3 lb) skinless chicken leg joints | 2 litres (3½ pints) water | 1 whole head of garlic | 100 g (3½ oz) Serrano ham, chopped | 1 tablespoon pimentón dulce (mild paprika) | 1 large onion, roughly chopped | 2 large carrots, roughly chopped | 4 celery sticks, roughly chopped | 100 g (3½ oz) finely shredded green cabbage | salt and freshly ground black pepper

ONE Soak the chickpeas in plenty of cold water overnight. Drain, rinse and put in a large, heavy-based saucepan with the chicken and measurement water. Bring to the boil, skimming off any foam that rises to the surface. **TWO** Add all the remaining ingredients, except the cabbage, and return to the boil. Reduce the heat to low, cover tightly and simmer gently for 1½ hours. The chickpeas should be tender and the chicken almost falling off the bone. **THREE** Only season to taste with salt and pepper now (the chickpeas will not soften if salt is added before they are tender) and add the cabbage. Bring to the boil and cook for 6–8 minutes. Ladle into warmed bowls and serve immediately.

Serves 4

NUTRIENT ANALYSIS PER SERVING 2419 kJ – 575 kcal – 56 g protein – 54 g carbohydrate – 10 g sugars – 17 g fat – 4 g saturates – 15 g fibre – 700 mg sodium

HEALTHY TIP Chickpeas are high in iron and dietary fibre and they are also a good source of protein. Carrots are useful for the betacarotenes they contain, which the body uses to make vitamin A. This vitamin is, among other things, essential for good vision.

CHICKEN WITH ORANGE AND MINT

Mint leaves and freshly squeezed orange juice flavour this chicken dish, which makes a special supper when served with sautéed potatoes and a salad, such as the Grilled Red Pepper Salad *(see page 104)* or Rice and Olive Salad *(see page 103)*.

INGREDIENTS 4 boneless, skinless chicken breasts, about 200 g (7 oz) each │ 3 tablespoons olive oil │ 150 ml (¼ pint) freshly squeezed orange juice │ 2 tablespoons chopped mint leaves, plus extra to garnish │ 1 tablespoon butter │ salt and freshly ground black pepper │ orange slices, to garnish

ONE Season the chicken breasts to taste with salt and pepper. Heat the oil in a large, nonstick frying pan, add the chicken breasts and cook over a medium heat, turning once, for 4–5 minutes or until golden all over. **TWO** Pour in the orange juice and bring to a simmer. Cover tightly, reduce the heat to low and cook gently for 8–10 minutes. **THREE** Add the chopped mint and butter and stir to mix well. Cook over a high heat, stirring, for 2 minutes. **FOUR** Serve the chicken immediately, garnished with chopped mint leaves and the orange slices.

Serves 4

NUTRIENT ANALYSIS PER SERVING 1454 kJ – 347 kcal – 44 g protein – 3 g carbohydrate – 3 g sugars – 18 g fat – 5 g saturates – 0 g fibre – 173 mg sodium

HEALTHY TIP Orange juice is a good source of vitamin C, although some will be lost in the cooking process as the vitamin is heat-sensitive. To reduce the salt in the recipe, use unsalted or slightly salted butter.

recipe illustrated on pages 160–161

LAMB WITH LEMON AND GARLIC

This simple and delicious lamb stew is from the Aragon region of north-eastern Spain. The lemon juice brings out the full flavour of the lamb, which is further enhanced by the addition of garlic and fresh parsley. Serve with Catalan-style Spinach *(see page 128)*.

INGREDIENTS 875 g (1¾ lb) lean boneless lamb, cut into bite-sized pieces │ 2 tablespoons olive oil │ 4 garlic cloves, crushed │ 1 onion, finely chopped │ 1 tablespoon pimentón dulce (mild paprika) │ 3 tablespoons lemon juice │ 4 tablespoons finely chopped flat leaf parsley, plus extra to garnish │ 100 ml (3½ fl oz) shop-bought or homemade Vegetable or Chicken Stock *(see pages 19–20)* │ salt and freshly ground black pepper │ finely grated lemon rind, to garnish

ONE Season the lamb to taste with salt and pepper. Heat the oil in a large, nonstick frying pan over a medium-high heat, add the lamb and cook, turning frequently, for 6–8 minutes until browned all over. **TWO** Transfer to a heavy-based, flameproof casserole and add the garlic, onion, pimentón, lemon juice, parsley and stock. Cover tightly and simmer gently over a low heat for 1½ hours or until the lamb is tender. Serve immediately, garnished with finely chopped parsley and grated lemon rind.

Serves 4

NUTRIENT ANALYSIS PER SERVING 1779 kJ – 425 kcal – 47 g protein – 4 g carbohydrate – 2 g sugars – 25 g fat – 10 g saturates – 1 g fibre – 196 mg sodium

HEALTHY TIP Lamb can be quite high in fat, depending on the cut of the meat. To keep down the fat content of this dish, use lean leg meat and cut off any visible fat.

recipe illustrated on pages 164–165

STUFFED ROASTED CHICKEN

This dish makes a great centrepiece for a Sunday lunch when served with mashed potatoes and a green or mixed salad. Or try serving it with the Sautéed Mushrooms *(see page 146)* or Griddled Asparagus *(see page 142)*. Choose a corn-fed chicken for the most delicious results.

INGREDIENTS 1 whole chicken, about 1.5 kg (3 lb) │ olive oil, for brushing │ salt and freshly ground black pepper

STUFFING 100 g (3½ oz) chorizo sausage, chopped │ 100 g (3½ oz) lean minced pork │ 4 tablespoons chopped flat leaf parsley │ 4 garlic cloves, crushed │ pinch of ground nutmeg │ 2 tablespoons finely chopped onion │ 1 tablespoon chopped oregano leaves │ finely grated rind and juice of 1 lemon │ 1 egg, beaten

ONE To make the stuffing, put all the ingredients in a bowl, season to taste with salt and pepper and, using your fingers, mix together until they are well combined. **TWO** Push the stuffing into the body cavity of the chicken and tie the legs together with fine kitchen string. Transfer the chicken to a roasting pan, lightly brush with oil and season to taste with salt and pepper. **THREE** Roast in a preheated oven, 200°C (400°F), Gas Mark 6, for 30 minutes. Reduce the oven temperature to 160°C (325°F), Gas Mark 3, and roast for a further 30–35 minutes or until the juices run clear when the chicken is pierced between the thigh and body. **FOUR** Remove from the oven, cover with foil and leave to rest in a warm place for 10–15 minutes. Carve and serve a little stuffing with each portion of chicken.

Serves 4

NUTRIENT ANALYSIS PER SERVING 2620 kJ – 630 kcal – 58 g protein – 3 g carbohydrate – 2 g sugars – 43 g fat – 13 g saturates – 1 g fibre – 350 mg sodium

HEALTHY TIP Most of the fat in a chicken is stored in the skin. To reduce the fat content of the dish, pour away any fat that collects in the roasting dish during the cooking process.

CHICKEN WITH RED PEPPERS

INGREDIENTS 4 tablespoons olive oil | 1 kg (2 lb) skinless chicken thighs | 4 garlic cloves, crushed | 1 onion, finely chopped | 50 g (2 oz) Serrano ham, diced | 3 red peppers, cored, deseeded and thinly sliced | 400 g (13 oz) can chopped tomatoes | 1 thyme sprig | 1 bay leaf | salt and freshly ground black pepper | chopped flat leaf parsley, to garnish

ONE Heat the oil in a large, heavy-based, shallow flameproof casserole, add the chicken, garlic and onion and cook them over a medium heat, turning frequently, for 4–5 minutes until the chicken is golden all over. **TWO** Add the ham and red peppers and cook, stirring, for 1–2 minutes. **THREE** Add the tomatoes and their juice, thyme sprig and bay leaf and bring to the boil. Reduce the heat to very low, cover tightly and cook for 1½ hours until the chicken is meltingly tender. **FOUR** Season to taste with salt and pepper, garnish with chopped parsley and serve.

Serves 4

NUTRIENT ANALYSIS PER SERVING 1535 kJ – 368 kcal – 34 g protein – 10 g carbohydrate – 9 g sugars – 21 g fat – 5 g saturates – 3 g fibre – 427 mg sodium

HEALTHY TIP The addition of Serrano ham to the chicken increases the sodium content of this dish. Taste the sauce before adding any extra salt.

VALENCIAN PAELLA

This typical Spanish midday dish has for its main ingredients rice, saffron and water. The remainder can be whatever comes to hand. This simplified version features chicken and chorizo, but prawns, mussels, clams and even snails are other favourite additions.

INGREDIENTS 1 kg (2 lb) skinless chicken thighs, cut into large pieces │ 4 tablespoons olive oil │ 200 g (7 oz) chorizo sausage, cut into 5 mm (¼ inch) slices │ 2 onions, finely chopped │ 4 garlic cloves, chopped │ 2 red peppers, cored, deseeded and finely chopped │ 700 g (1 lb 6 oz) paella rice, such as Calasparra or Bomba │ 3 tablespoons finely chopped flat leaf parsley, plus extra to garnish │ 1 bay leaf │ a large pinch of saffron threads │ 1.5 litres (2½ pints) shop-bought or homemade Chicken Stock *(see page 20)* │ 100 g (3½ oz) fresh or frozen peas │ 100 g (3½ oz) shelled fresh or frozen broad beans │ salt and freshly ground black pepper

ONE Pat the chicken dry with kitchen paper and season to taste with salt and pepper. Heat the oil in a *paellera* or a heavy-based, shallow flameproof casserole over a medium-high heat, add the chicken and cook, turning frequently, for 4–5 minutes until it is golden all over. Remove with a slotted spoon to a plate and keep warm. **TWO** Add the chorizo to the pan with the onions, garlic and red peppers and cook, stirring frequently, for 4–5 minutes. **THREE** Return the chicken and any juices that have accumulated to the pan and stir in the rice, parsley, bay leaf and saffron. Stir in the stock, peas and broad beans, bring to a simmer and cook over a low heat, uncovered, for 12–15 minutes. **FOUR** Reduce the heat to very low, cover tightly and cook for a further 12–15 minutes until the rice is tender and all the liquid has been absorbed. **FIVE** Remove the pan from the heat and leave to stand, covered, for 10 minutes before serving the paella, garnished with chopped parsley.

Serves 6–8

NUTRIENT ANALYSIS PER SERVING 3145 kJ – 746 kcal – 33 g protein – 113 g carbohydrate – 7 g sugars – 21 g fat – 6 g saturates – 5 g fibre – 277 mg sodium

HEALTHY TIP Rice and meat are combined to make a nutritious dish, high in protein and quite low in fat. Broad beans and peas are great sources of fibre, and peppers and onions provide protective antioxidants.

recipe illustrated on pages 172–173

BASQUE-STYLE DUCK

Basque cooking is renowned for its excellence and often produces the simplest and most delicious Spanish food. This dish is a prime example.

INGREDIENTS 1 teaspoon pimentón dulce (mild paprika) │ pinch of ground cloves │ 1 teaspoon ground cinnamon │ 4 large duck breasts, about 275 g (9 oz) each │ 3 tablespoons olive oil │ 6 spring onions, finely chopped │ 2 garlic cloves, crushed │ 2 tablespoons plain flour │ 100 ml (3½ fl oz) sweet sherry │ 200 ml (7 fl oz) shop-bought or homemade Chicken Stock *(see page 20)* │ 4 tablespoons finely chopped tarragon, plus a sprig to garnish │ 1 thyme sprig │ salt and freshly ground black pepper

ONE Rub the spices over the duck, and season with salt and pepper. **TWO** Heat a large frying pan over a high heat, then add the oil and heat. Add the duck and cook for 2–3 minutes on each side until lightly browned. Transfer to a baking sheet with a slotted spoon. Roast in a preheated oven, 180°C (350°F), Gas Mark 4, for 15–20 minutes. **THREE** Meanwhile, heat the frying pan, add the spring onions and garlic and cook, stirring, for 1–2 minutes. Add the flour and cook, stirring constantly, for 30–40 seconds. Pour in the sherry and cook for 1–2 minutes, then add the stock. Bring to the boil, stirring, then reduce the heat and add the herbs. Simmer for 4–5 minutes. **FOUR** Remove the duck from the oven and add to the pan. Toss to coat with the sauce, adjust the seasoning, and serve immediately, garnished with a sprig of tarragon.

Serves 4

NUTRIENT ANALYSIS PER SERVING 1069 kJ – 256 kcal – 17 g protein – 11 g carbohydrate – 2 g sugars – 14 g fat – 3 g saturates – 0 g fibre – 90 mg sodium

HEALTHY TIP Duck is quite high in fat, but much of this is in the skin or just under it and will run out in the roasting process. Use a slotted spoon to transfer the duck, to allow as much of the fat as possible to be poured away.

MADRID-STYLE PORK

In this easy recipe, lean pork fillet is marinated with herbs and spices and then simply grilled. Serve with steamed greens or the Spanish-style Green Beans *(see page 123)* and boiled potatoes.

INGREDIENTS 3 garlic cloves, crushed | 1 tablespoon pimentón dulce (mild paprika) | 1 teaspoon dried oregano | 1 teaspoon chopped thyme leaves | 2 tablespoons olive oil | 500 g (1 lb) pork fillet | salt and freshly ground black pepper

ONE Mix the garlic, pimentón, oregano, thyme and oil together in a small bowl and season to taste with salt and pepper. **TWO** Put the pork in a shallow dish and rub the herb and spice mixture all over. Cover with clingfilm and leave to marinate overnight in the refrigerator, turning the pork occasionally. **THREE** When ready to cook, remove the pork from the refrigerator and leave to return to room temperature. Slice the pork into 1.5 cm (¾ inch) thick rounds. **FOUR** Heat a griddle pan over a high heat until smoking, add the pork, in batches, and cook for 2–3 minutes on each side or until cooked to your liking, but do not overcook. Remove from the pan and keep warm while cooking the remaining pork. Serve hot.

Serves 4

NUTRIENT ANALYSIS PER SERVING 987 kJ – 237 kcal – 26 g protein – 1 g carbohydrate – 0 g sugars – 15 g fat – 4 g saturates – 0 g fibre – 70 mg sodium

HEALTHY TIP Although there is some fat running through the meat, giving it texture and flavour, pork is a leaner meat today than in the past. Choose a lean cut and remove any visible fat.

RABBIT WITH WILD MUSHROOMS

Rabbit is a popular ingredient in Spanish cooking, as are mushrooms harvested from the countryside – usually flat, brown mushrooms called *rovellones*. Cooked in full-bodied red wine, they make a memorable duo in this rich stew. Serve with hot mashed potatoes and carrots, or try serving it with the Spring Vegetable Stew *(see page 124)*.

INGREDIENTS 3 tablespoons olive oil | 1 kg (2 lb) whole rabbit, cut into large pieces | 2 onions, finely chopped | 4 garlic cloves, finely chopped | 200 g (7 oz) Serrano ham, sliced | 300 ml (½ pint) Rioja or other robust red wine | 250 g (8 oz) wild mushrooms, thickly sliced | salt and freshly ground black pepper | finely chopped flat leaf parsley, to garnish

ONE Heat the oil in a large, flameproof casserole over a medium-high heat, add the rabbit and cook, turning frequently, for 4–5 minutes until browned all over. Remove with a slotted spoon to a plate and keep warm. **TWO** Add the onions and garlic to the casserole and cook over a low heat, stirring frequently, for 5–6 minutes until the onions are softened. **THREE** Increase the heat to high, add the ham and cook, stirring, for 3–4 minutes. Return the rabbit and any juices that have accumulated to the casserole. Pour over the wine, season to taste with salt and pepper and bring to the boil. Reduce the heat to low, cover tightly and cook for 40 minutes. **FOUR** Add the mushrooms and stir to mix well. Re-cover and cook for a further 12–15 minutes. Serve immediately, garnished with the parsley.

Serves 4

NUTRIENT ANALYSIS PER SERVING 1943 kJ – 319 kcal – 50 g protein – 7 g carbohydrate – 5 g sugars – 21 g fat – 6 g saturates – 3 g fibre – 1117 mg sodium

HEALTHY TIP Rabbit is low in fat. The Serrano ham increases the sodium content of the recipe considerably, so taste the sauce before seasoning with extra salt.

recipe illustrated on pages 180–181

LENTILS AND CHORIZO STEW

Brown lentils are widely used in Spain in soups and salads as well as stews, such as this robust one, and they don't require any presoaking. This makes an easy, filling dish for entertaining. Serve with chunks of warm crusty bread.

INGREDIENTS 250 g (8 oz) brown lentils, washed and drained │ 1 leek, trimmed, cleaned and thinly sliced │ 2 onions, finely chopped │ 2 carrots, finely diced │ 2 garlic cloves, finely chopped │ 250 g (8 oz) chorizo sausage, finely chopped or sliced │ 1 tablespoon pimentón dulce (mild paprika) │ 2 tablespoons olive oil │ salt and freshly ground black pepper

ONE Put the lentils in a large saucepan and cover with cold water (about 500 ml/17 fl oz). Add the leek and one of the onions, the carrots, garlic, chorizo and pimentón and season to taste with salt and pepper. Add half the oil and bring to a simmer. **TWO** Cover and cook over a very low heat for 45–50 minutes or until the lentils are tender. The mixture should be quite thick. **THREE** Meanwhile, heat the remaining oil in a small frying pan, add the remaining onion and cook over a medium heat, stirring frequently, for 10–12 minutes until lightly browned. Stir into the lentil stew and serve immediately.

Serves 4

NUTRIENT ANALYSIS PER SERVING 1983 kJ – 473 kcal – 28 g protein – 44 g carbohydrate – 11 g sugars – 22 g fat – 7 g saturates – 8 g fibre – 380 mg sodium

HEALTHY TIP Lentils are a good source of protein and also contain significant amounts of iron, which boosts the immune system and is essential for healthy blood.

recipe illustrated on pages 184–185

BAKED EGGS WITH CHORIZO, HAM AND ASPARAGUS

This well-known Andalusian dish, originating from Seville, is very colourful to look at and makes a welcome lunch or supper dish.

INGREDIENTS 2 tablespoons olive oil │ 1 onion, finely chopped │ 3 garlic cloves, finely chopped │ 400 g (13 oz) can chopped tomatoes │ 1 teaspoon golden caster sugar │ 1 teaspoon pimentón dulce (mild paprika) │ 2 canned pimientos, drained and cut into thick strips │ 12 asparagus tips │ 100 g (3½ oz) fresh or frozen peas │ 4 eggs │ 100 g (3½ oz) chorizo sausage, roughly chopped │ 100 g (3½ oz) Serrano ham, finely diced │ salt and freshly ground black pepper │ finely chopped flat leaf parsley, to garnish

ONE Heat the oil in a large frying pan, add the onion and garlic and cook over a medium heat, stirring frequently, for 10 minutes until the onion is soft. Add the tomatoes and their juice, sugar and pimentón and cook over a high heat, stirring occasionally, for 10 minutes. Season to taste with salt and pepper, then transfer the mixture to a shallow, round ovenproof dish, about 25 cm (10 inches) in diameter. **TWO** Add the pimientos, asparagus and peas and stir well. Make 4 indentations in the mixture and break an egg into each. **THREE** Bake in a preheated oven, 200°C (400°F), Gas Mark 6, for 8–10 minutes or until the eggs are just set. Remove from the oven and keep warm. **FOUR** Heat a dry frying pan until very hot, add the chorizo and ham and cook over a high heat, stirring, for 4–5 minutes until well browned and crisp. Spoon the chorizo and ham over the top of the vegetables and serve immediately, garnished with parsley.

Serves 4

NUTRIENT ANALYSIS PER SERVING 1330 kJ – 319 kcal – 22 g protein – 15 g carbohydrate – 12 g sugars – 19 g fat – 5 g saturates – 5 g fibre – 740 mg sodium

HEALTHY TIP Eggs do contain cholesterol, but they are nutritious and can be safely eaten in moderation. Asparagus is a good source of folic acid, necessary for the formation of new cells in the body.

recipe illustrated on pages 188–189

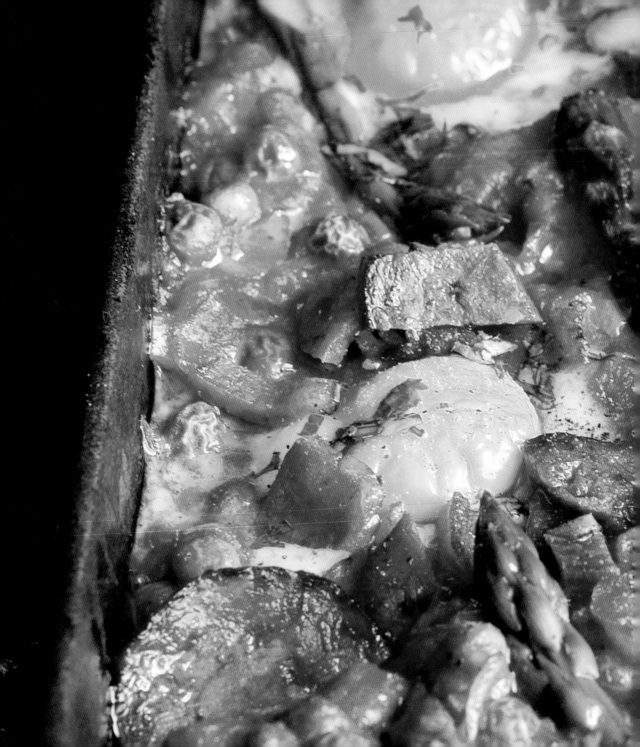

CATALAN-STYLE NOODLES WITH PORK SAUSAGES

Fideus – *fideos* in Spanish – is short, thin Spanish pasta, very similar to Italian vermicelli, and was introduced to Catalonia by the Moors. In this dish, spicy fresh pork sausages are cooked with garlic, onions and tomatoes to create a wonderfully hearty main course.

INGREDIENTS 4 tablespoons olive oil | 625 g (1¼ lb) large fresh pork sausages | 1 large onion, finely chopped | 4 garlic cloves, finely chopped | 400 g (13 oz) can tomatoes | 1 teaspoon pimentón dulce (mild paprika) | 250 g (8 oz) fideus pasta or vermicelli, cut into short lengths | 1 litre (1¾ pints) shop-bought or homemade Chicken or Vegetable Stock *(see pages 19–20)* | salt and freshly ground black pepper | chopped flat leaf parsley, to garnish

ONE Heat half the oil in a 25 cm (10 inch) shallow flameproof casserole or frying pan with a lid and an ovenproof handle. Add the sausages and cook over a medium-high heat, turning frequently, for 3–4 minutes or until lightly browned all over. Remove with a slotted spoon and set aside. **TWO** Heat the remaining oil in the pan, add the onion and garlic and cook over a low heat, stirring occasionally, for 10 minutes until soft. Add the tomatoes and their juice and pimentón and cook over a medium heat, stirring, for 3–4 minutes. Return the sausages to the pan with the pasta and stock. Season to taste with salt and pepper, stir to mix well and bring to the boil. **THREE** Cover the casserole or frying pan and cook in a preheated oven, 190°C (375°C), Gas Mark 5, for 20–25 minutes or until most of the liquid has been absorbed. **FOUR** Remove from the oven and sprinkle over the chopped parsley to garnish before serving straight from the casserole or pan.

Serves 4

NUTRIENT ANALYSIS PER SERVING 2814 kJ – 670 kcal – 23 g protein – 66 g carbohydrate – 10 g sugars – 37 g fat – 11 g saturates – 6 g fibre – 1090 mg sodium

HEALTHY TIP Most sausages have quite a high salt content, so you won't need to add much salt to the pasta and stock during cooking. Combining meat with a starchy food such as pasta, potatoes or rice improves the protein quality of the dish.

recipe illustrated on pages 192–193

FISH AND

SEAFOOD

SPANISH RICE WITH CLAMS AND VEGETABLES

Creamy rice and sweet clams are perfectly combined in this colourful dish, with the addition of plenty of fresh vegetables.

INGREDIENTS 4 tablespoons olive oil │ 1 small red onion, finely chopped │ 1 small leek, thinly sliced │ 1 carrot, cut into 1 cm (½ inch) dice │ 100 g (3½ oz) green beans, trimmed and cut into 1 cm (½ inch) lengths │ 1 large tomato, skinned, deseeded and diced │ 400 g (13 oz) paella rice, such as Calasparra or Bomba │ 2 garlic cloves, crushed │ 20–25 live clams, prepared *(see page 16)* │ 2 tablespoons tomato purée │ 1 tablespoon pimentón dulce (mild paprika) │ 150 ml (¼ pint) dry white wine │ 1 tablespoon chopped flat leaf parsley, plus extra to garnish │ salt and freshly ground black pepper

ONE Heat half the oil in a large, nonstick frying pan, add the onion, leek, carrot and green beans and cook over a medium heat for 6–8 minutes until softened. Add the tomato and cook for 2–3 minutes. **TWO** Rinse the rice and drain. Add to the pan and cook, stirring, for 2–3 minutes. Add enough water to cover the rice and vegetables and slowly bring to the boil. **THREE** Meanwhile, heat the remaining oil in a saucepan, add the garlic and cook over a medium heat, stirring, for 1–2 minutes. Add the drained clams with the tomato purée, pimentón, wine and parsley. Cover tightly and cook over a high heat, shaking the pan vigorously several times, for 4–5 minutes or until all the clams have opened (discard any that remain closed). **FOUR** Transfer the clams to the rice, mix well and cook for a further 8–10 minutes or until the rice is just tender. Season with salt and pepper, garnish with chopped parsley and serve immediately.

Serves 4

NUTRIENT ANALYSIS PER SERVING 2320 kJ – 550 kcal – 13 g protein – 96 g carbohydrate – 6 g sugars – 13 g fat – 2 g saturates – 5 g fibre – 66 mg sodium

HEALTHY TIP As well as containing valuable omega-3 fatty acids, which are believed to have a protective effect against coronary heart disease, clams also provide minerals that are vital for wellbeing, such as iron, zinc and selenium.

GALICIAN-STYLE MONKFISH

This delicious fish dish from Galicia in north-western Spain uses golden saffron and sweet almonds to flavour it. You could use any firm white fish fillets instead of the monkfish if you prefer. Serve with a mixed salad, or try the Leek Salad *(see page 114)* as an accompaniment.

INGREDIENTS 800 g (1 lb 10 oz) monkfish fillet, skinned │ 1 onion, very finely chopped │ olive oil, for drizzling │ 15 whole blanched almonds, toasted and finely ground │ 3 garlic cloves, crushed │ a large pinch of saffron threads, crushed │ 1 tablespoon finely chopped flat leaf parsley │ 2–3 tablespoons water │ 250 g (8 oz) fresh or frozen peas │ salt and freshly ground black pepper

ONE Cut the monkfish into 8 evenly-sized pieces. Spread the onion out over the base of a medium-sized flameproof casserole and arrange the monkfish over the top. Season to taste with salt and pepper and drizzle over a little oil. Cover tightly and cook over a medium heat for 5–6 minutes. **TWO** Meanwhile, put the ground almonds, garlic, saffron and parsley in a small bowl with the measurement water and blend together to make a smooth paste. **THREE** Spread the mixture over the top of the fish and add the peas. Re-cover and cook for a further 4–5 minutes or until the fish is cooked through. Serve immediately.

Serves 4

NUTRIENT ANALYSIS PER SERVING 1048 kJ – 248 kcal – 37 g protein – 10 g carbohydrate – 4 g sugars – 7 g fat – 1 g saturates – 6 g fibre – 40 mg sodium

HEALTHY TIP Monkfish is a very low-fat fish, so most of the small amount of fat in this recipe comes from the almonds and olive oil. Both of these are rich in beneficial monounsaturated fat. Onions and garlic may help to avert coronary heart disease by lowering the risk of blood clots forming.

recipe illustrated on pages 202–203

BAKED SARDINES

Sardines are particularly valued by the Spanish, but they must be absolutely fresh and firm, not tired or limp. Ask your fish supplier to fillet the fish but keep them whole, so that they can be opened out like a book to season and then closed up again to cook and serve. Here, they are baked with a spiced tomato mixture and are equally good served at room temperature. Either way, serve with warm crusty bread.

INGREDIENTS 3 tablespoons olive oil │ 2 onions, finely chopped │ 4 garlic cloves, crushed │ 1 red pepper, cored, deseeded and finely chopped │ 200 g (7 oz) can chopped tomatoes │ 1 teaspoon pimentón picante (hot paprika) │ a large pinch of saffron threads │ ½ teaspoon ground cumin │ 1 bay leaf │ 1 cinnamon stick │ 3 tablespoons finely chopped flat leaf parsley, plus extra to garnish │ 12 medium or 20–25 small fresh whole sardines, prepared *(see page 16)* and filleted but kept whole │ salt and freshly ground black pepper

ONE Heat the oil in a large frying pan, add the onions, garlic and red pepper and cook over a low heat, stirring occasionally, for 10–15 minutes. **TWO** Add the tomatoes and their juice, pimentón, saffron, cumin, bay leaf, cinnamon stick and parsley, season to taste with salt and pepper and cook, stirring occasionally, for a further 8–10 minutes. **THREE** Gently open out the sardine fillets and lightly season with salt and pepper. Fold back into their original shape. Spread half the tomato mixture over the base of a medium-sized, shallow ovenproof dish or *cazuela (see page 15)*. Arrange half the sardines on top in a single layer. Repeat with the remaining tomato mixture and sardines. **FOUR** Bake in a preheated oven, 200°C (400°F), Gas Mark 6, for 15–20 minutes or until the fish is cooked through. Remove from the oven and serve immediately, garnished with a little finely chopped parsley.

Serves 4–6

NUTRIENT ANALYSIS PER SERVING 1544 kJ – 370 kcal – 33 g protein – 10 g carbohydrate – 8 g sugars – 23 g fat – 5 g saturates – 2 g fibre – 203 mg sodium

HEALTHY TIP A fatty fish, sardines are a convenient source of polyunsaturated fatty acids. These are thought to be particularly important in the maintenance of 'good' HDL cholesterol in the blood and the prevention of heart disease.

recipe illustrated on pages 206–207

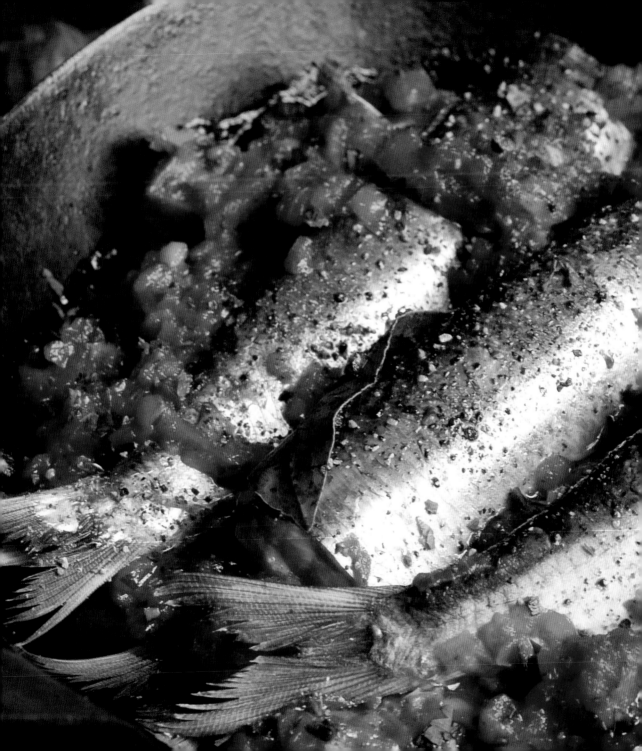

PICKLED MACKEREL

In this wonderfully simple recipe, mackerel fillets are left to marinate overnight in a herbed and spiced vinegar. They taste even better if eaten 2–3 days later (store in an airtight container in the refrigerator). You can use fresh sardine fillets instead of mackerel.

INGREDIENTS 800 g (1 lb 10 oz) mackerel fillets │ 4 tablespoons plain flour │ 1 tablespoon pimentón dulce (mild paprika) │ 1 teaspoon sea salt │ 2 tablespoons olive oil │ 2 garlic cloves, finely chopped │ 1 small red onion, cut into thin rings │ 1 small carrot, cut into small dice │ 4 tablespoons finely chopped flat leaf parsley │ 1 teaspoon chopped oregano leaves │ 1 bay leaf │ 6 black peppercorns │ 6 tablespoons white wine vinegar │ 4 tablespoons water

ONE Cut the mackerel fillets into large pieces. Put the flour on a plate with the pimentón and salt and mix together. Dust the fish pieces with the seasoned flour. **TWO** Heat the oil in a large, nonstick frying pan, add the fish and cook for 1–2 minutes on each side. Remove from the pan with a slotted spoon and put in a shallow, non-reactive heatproof dish in a single layer. **THREE** Add the garlic, onion and carrot to the pan with the parsley, oregano, bay leaf and peppercorns. Pour in the vinegar and measurement water and bring to the boil. Remove from the heat and pour the mixture over the fish. **FOUR** Leave to cool, then cover and leave to marinate overnight in the refrigerator before serving.

Serves 4

NUTRIENT ANALYSIS PER SERVING 2412 kJ – 580 kcal – 40 g protein – 19 g carbohydrate – 3 g sugars – 39 g fat – 7 g saturates – 2 g fibre – 760 mg sodium

HEALTHY TIP Mackerel is a particularly good source of omega-3 fat, which is believed to lower triglycerides (blood fats), reduce the risk of blood clotting and protect against coronary heart disease.

recipe illustrated on pages 210–211

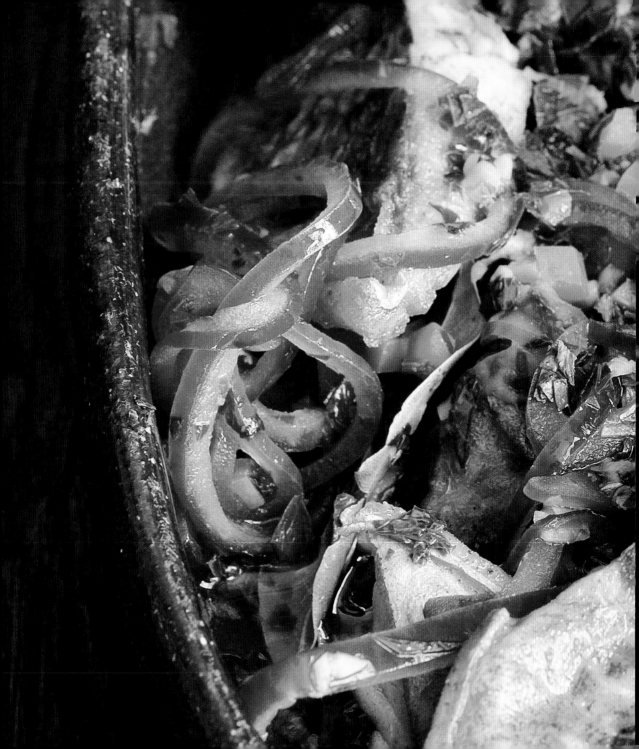

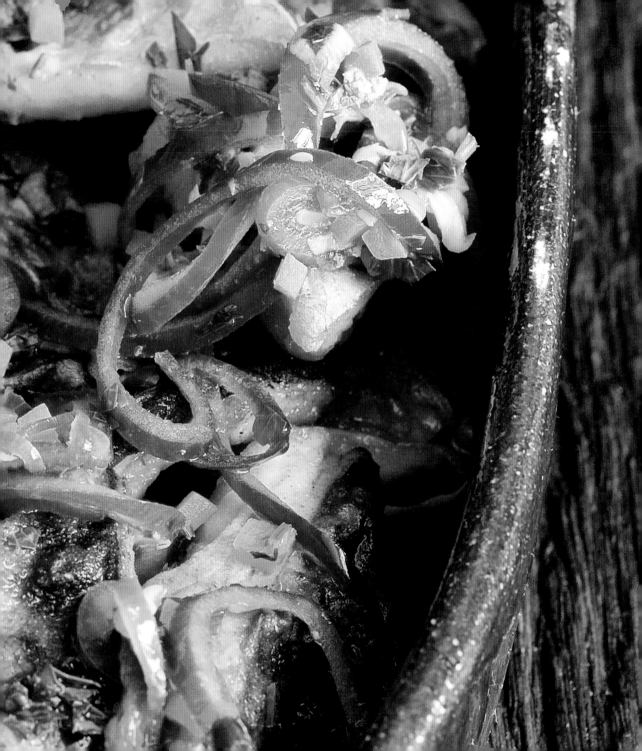

STUFFED BABY SQUID

INGREDIENTS 800 g (1 lb 10 oz) small or baby squid, prepared *(see page 16)* | 6 spring onions, very finely chopped | 50 g (2 oz) toasted pine nuts | 50 g (2 oz) raisins | 2 small eggs, lightly beaten | 100 g (3½ oz) fresh white breadcrumbs | 1 teaspoon ground cinnamon | 200 ml (7 fl oz) white wine | 200 ml (7 fl oz) shop-bought or homemade Vegetable Stock *(see page 19)* | a large pinch of saffron threads | olive oil, for drizzling | salt and freshly ground black pepper

ONE Finely chop about 4–5 tablespoonfuls of the squid tentacles and put in a bowl (the remainder can be used in a fish stew). **TWO** Add the spring onions, pine nuts, raisins, eggs and breadcrumbs to the tentacles and mix together to form a relatively firm mixture. Add the cinnamon and season to taste with salt and pepper. **THREE** Stuff the squid body cavities with the mixture and arrange in a single layer in a large *cazuela (see page 15)* or large, shallow flameproof casserole. Pour over the wine and stock, sprinkle over the saffron and drizzle with a little oil. **FOUR** Bring to the boil, then reduce the heat to low and simmer, uncovered, for 25–30 minutes, turning the squid over occasionally, until tender. Serve immediately.

Serves 4

NUTRIENT ANALYSIS PER SERVING 1730 kJ – 413 kcal – 38 g protein – 24 g carbohydrate – 11 g sugars – 15 g fat – 2 g saturates – 2 g fibre – 526 mg sodium

HEALTHY TIP Adding raisins, pine nuts and eggs gives this dish a higher iron content.

GRILLED SCALLOPS

This grilled scallop dish makes a perfect supper served with a mixed salad or the Red Onion and Orange Salad *(see page 109)*, and crusty bread. If you don't want to prepare the scallops yourself, ask your fish supplier to do it for you and give you the shells.

INGREDIENTS 12 raw scallops, prepared *(see page 16)*, 8 shells reserved │ 1 garlic clove, very finely chopped │ 1 tablespoon very finely chopped shallot │ 2 tablespoons very finely chopped tomato │ ¼ teaspoon finely grated lemon rind │ 1 tablespoon lemon juice │ 2 tablespoons very finely chopped flat leaf parsley │ 3 tablespoons fresh white breadcrumbs │ olive oil, for drizzling │ salt and freshly ground black pepper

ONE Roughly chop the scallops and put in a bowl. Add the garlic, shallot, tomato, lemon rind and juice and parsley. Season to taste with salt and pepper and mix well to combine. **TWO** Divide the scallop mixture between the scallop shells and sprinkle over the breadcrumbs. Drizzle with a little oil. **THREE** Cook under a preheated medium-high grill for 6–8 minutes or until lightly golden and the scallops are just cooked through. Serve immediately.

Serves 4

NUTRIENT ANALYSIS PER SERVING 580 kJ – 137 kcal – 19 g protein – 10 g carbohydrate – 1 g sugars – 3 g fat – 1 g saturates – 1 g fibre – 200 mg sodium

HEALTHY TIP Scallops contain useful amounts of trace minerals such as copper and selenium, as well as small amounts of B vitamins. They are also low in fat. In general, low-fat fish contain less vitamins and minerals than the fatty fish, but all low-fat fish make a very healthy source of protein.

recipe illustrated on pages 216–217

BAKED CRABS BASQUE STYLE

Txangurro is the Basque name for the big spider or spiny crabs found in the Bay of Biscay. This recipe uses regular crabs, available from any quality fish supplier. If you can't find whole crabs, use about 400 g (13 oz) cooked crabmeat and bake in individual ovenproof dishes.

INGREDIENTS 4 whole freshly cooked crabs | 2 tablespoons olive oil, plus extra for drizzling | 2 onions, finely chopped | 2 garlic cloves, finely chopped | 2 ripe tomatoes, skinned, deseeded and finely chopped | 4 tablespoons chopped flat leaf parsley, plus extra to garnish | 100 ml (3½ fl oz) dry white wine | 100 ml (3½ fl oz) shop-bought or homemade Fish or Vegetable Stock *(see pages 21 and 19)* | 1 teaspoon pimentón dulce (mild paprika) | 2 tablespoons fresh white breadcrumbs | salt and freshly ground black pepper

ONE Pick out all the meat from the cooked crabs and set aside. Wash the crab shells, pat them dry and set them aside on a baking sheet. **TWO** Heat the oil in a large, nonstick frying pan, add the onions and garlic and cook over a low heat, stirring occasionally, for 10–12 minutes until the onions are very soft. **THREE** Add the tomatoes and cook over a medium heat, stirring frequently, for 10 minutes. Add the parsley, wine and stock and season to taste with salt and pepper. Cook for 3–4 minutes, then add the pimentón and crabmeat. Cook, stirring, for 3–4 minutes. **FOUR** Pack the mixture into the crab shells, sprinkle over the breadcrumbs and drizzle with oil. Bake in a preheated oven, 200°C (400°F), Gas Mark 6, for 8–10 minutes or until the tops are just lightly browned. Serve immediately, garnished with chopped parsley.

Serves 4

NUTRIENT ANALYSIS PER SERVING 1360 kJ – 325 kcal – 32 g protein – 12 g carbohydrate – 6 g sugars – 15 g fat – 2 g saturates – 2 g fibre – 600 mg sodium

HEALTHY TIP Crab is an excellent low-fat source of protein. It also contains small amounts of B vitamins and a number of trace minerals, such as copper, zinc and selenium.

TRADITIONAL FISH AND POTATO STEW

This robust one-pot fish stew from the Basque region gets its Spanish name *Marmita-kua* from the utensil that it is traditionally cooked in – a *marmita*. You can use any firm fresh fish in place of the tuna.

INGREDIENTS 800 g (1 lb 10 oz) tuna fillets, cut into large bite-sized pieces │ 4 tablespoons olive oil │ 2 red onions, halved and thinly sliced │ 4 garlic cloves, thinly sliced │ 3 ripe tomatoes, skinned, deseeded and chopped │ 2 bay leaves │ 1 red pepper, cored, deseeded and diced │ 1 tablespoon pimentón dulce (mild paprika) │ 625 g (1¼ lb) potatoes, peeled and cut into large bite-sized pieces │ salt and freshly ground black pepper

TO GARNISH chopped flat leaf parsley │ capers

ONE Arrange the tuna in a shallow bowl in a single layer and season to taste with salt and pepper. Cover and set aside. **TWO** Heat the oil in a medium-sized saucepan, add the onions and garlic and cook over a medium heat, stirring frequently, for 8–10 minutes until soft. **THREE** Add the tomatoes, bay leaves, red pepper, pimentón and potatoes and stir to mix well. Add enough water to just cover all the ingredients and bring to the boil. Reduce the heat and simmer gently for 25–30 minutes or until the potatoes are tender. **FOUR** Add the fish, return to the boil and cook for 4–5 minutes. **FIVE** Taste and adjust the seasoning if necessary, then serve ladled into warmed shallow bowls, garnished with chopped parsley and capers.

Serves 4

NUTRIENT ANALYSIS PER SERVING 2299 kJ – 547 kcal – 53 g protein – 39 g carbohydrate – 11 g sugars – 21 g fat – 4 g saturates – 6 g fibre – 119 mg sodium

HEALTHY TIP Tuna is a low-fat fish and an excellent source of protein. Like many fish, it contains useful amounts of selenium, which is necessary for a healthy thyroid. The combination of tuna with potatoes, tomatoes and onions makes this a particularly nutritious dish.

recipe illustrated on pages 222–223

MIXED FISH STEW

The Spanish name for this dish, *zarzuela*, actually means a light opera in Spain. But in this context it signifies a sublime mixture of fresh fish and shellfish, cooked in white wine. You can vary the ingredients and proportions to whatever combination you desire.

INGREDIENTS 2 tablespoons olive oil | 12 raw tiger prawns in their shells | 1 onion, finely chopped | 4 garlic cloves, crushed | 2 ripe tomatoes, chopped | 1 bay leaf | a large pinch of saffron threads | 1 teaspoon pimentón dulce (mild paprika) | 1 dried red chilli | 250 ml (8 fl oz) dry white wine | 400 g (13 oz) firm white fish fillets, such as cod or halibut, cut into bite-sized pieces | 4 small squid, prepared *(see page 16)* and sliced | 6 live mussels, prepared *(see page 16)* | 1 tablespoon ground almonds | 3 tablespoons finely chopped flat leaf parsley, plus extra whole leaves to garnish | salt and freshly ground black pepper

ONE Heat the oil in a large, shallow flameproof casserole, add the whole prawns and cook over a high heat until they turn pink. Remove with a slotted spoon to a plate and set aside. Add the onion and half the garlic and cook over a low heat, stirring occasionally, for 10 minutes until the onion is soft. **TWO** Add the tomatoes, bay leaf, saffron, pimentón, chilli and wine and bring to the boil. Add the fish and squid and cook, stirring occasionally, for 5 minutes, then add the mussels and cook, stirring occasionally, for 4–5 minutes or until they have all opened (discard any that remain closed). **THREE** Mix the ground almonds with the remaining garlic and the parsley and stir into the casserole. Season to taste with salt and pepper and return the prawns with any juices that have accumulated to the casserole. Stir to mix well, then ladle into warmed shallow soup plates and serve immediately, garnished with a few parsley leaves.

Serves 4–6

NUTRIENT ANALYSIS PER SERVING 1310 kJ – 313 kcal – 40 g protein – 6 g carbohydrate – 4 g sugars – 10 g fat – 1 g saturates – 2 g fibre – 340 mg sodium

HEALTHY TIP A hearty fish stew that is low in fat and high in protein. Tomatoes contain the antioxidant lycopene, which studies suggest may have a role in preventing cancer by suppressing the growth of tumours and inactivating carcinogens.

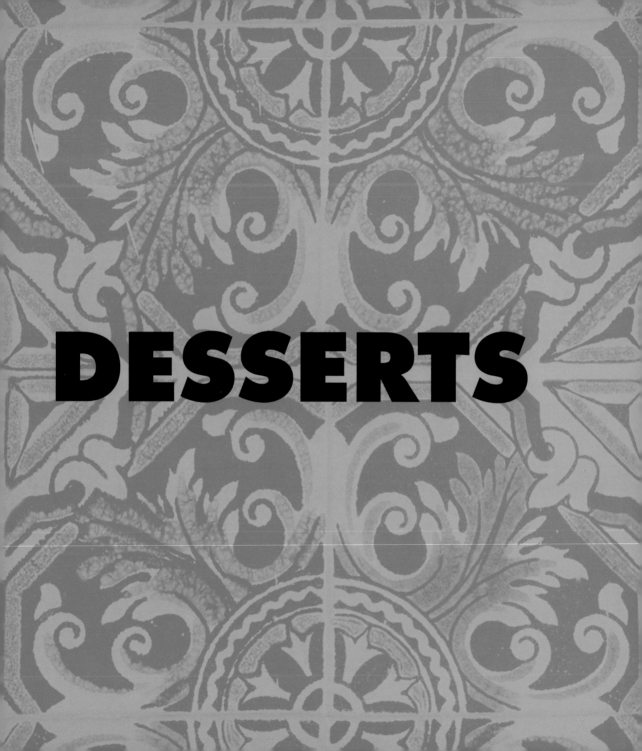

DESSERTS

PEACHES IN WINE

INGREDIENTS 4 ripe peaches | 350 ml (12 fl oz) dry red wine | 75 g (3 oz) golden caster sugar | 4 thin slices of lemon, pips removed | 1 cinnamon stick, plus extra pieces to garnish | 350 ml (12 fl oz) water | crème fraîche, to serve (optional)

ONE Bring a large saucepan of water to the boil. Add the peaches and leave for 30 seconds. Drain and plunge into cold water, then peel away the skins. **TWO** Put the peaches in a saucepan large enough to hold them in a single layer and add the wine, sugar, lemon slices, cinnamon and measurement water. Bring to a simmer, cover and cook for 12–15 minutes or until tender. **THREE** Remove the peaches with a slotted spoon and transfer to a shallow heatproof serving dish. Boil the remaining liquid in the saucepan over a high heat for 6–8 minutes or until reduced and syrupy. Remove from the heat and pour over the peaches. **FOUR** Leave to cool, then cover and chill in the refrigerator for 2 hours. Serve the peaches in individual bowls or on plates with the syrup drizzled over and a dollop of crème fraîche, if you like. Garnish each serving with a piece of cinnamon stick.

Serves 4

NUTRIENT ANALYSIS PER SERVING 720 kJ – 170 kcal – 1 g protein – 28 g carbohydrate – 28 g sugars – 0 g fat – 0 g saturates – 3 g fibre – 10 mg sodium

HEALTHY TIP Peaches contain vitamins C and B, as well as carotene, the precursor to vitamin A. These vitamins help maintain a healthy immune system, while carotene and vitamin C are important antioxidants, which are thought to have a role in the prevention of cancer.

SPANISH CUSTARD CREAMS

These creamy cinnamon-flavoured custards are perfect to follow a spicy main course. You can add finely grated orange or lemon rind to the mixture for added flavour if you like.

INGREDIENTS 750 ml (1¼ pints) semi-skimmed milk │ 1 cinnamon stick │ 6 egg yolks │ 150 g (5 oz) golden caster sugar │ 2 teaspoons cornflour │ ground cinnamon, for dusting │ sweet biscuits, to serve (optional)

ONE Bring all but 50 ml (2 fl oz) of the milk and cinnamon stick to the boil in a saucepan over a medium heat. Meanwhile, beat the egg yolks and sugar with an electric whisk in a large bowl until light and frothy. **TWO** Blend the cornflour with the remaining milk in a cup, then add to the egg yolk mixture. Beat well to combine. **THREE** When the milk comes to the boil, remove from the heat and remove the cinnamon stick. Gradually add the egg mixture, stirring constantly, and then return the pan to a very low heat and cook, stirring constantly, until the custard thickens. Remove from the heat and leave to cool before spooning into individual bowls or dessert glasses. **FOUR** Cover and chill for 2–3 hours or overnight. Lightly dust with ground cinnamon before serving, accompanied by sweet biscuits, if you like.

Serves 4

NUTRIENT ANALYSIS PER SERVING 1412 kJ – 334 kcal – 11 g protein – 51 g carbohydrate – 49 g sugars – 11 g fat – 4 g saturates – 0 g fibre – 46 mg sodium

HEALTHY TIP These custards are very rich in calcium and they also contain egg yolks, high in vitamin D. This vitamin plays a vital role in maintaining bone calcium levels. A diet rich in vitamin D is essential for the house-bound, or anyone who is not able to expose their skin to sunlight.

recipe illustrated on pages 234–235

STUFFED FIGS

Summertime in Spain sees a glut of this luscious fruit, which has over 60 varieties. As the abundant harvest cannot all be eaten fresh, many are dried, and this recipe makes excellent use of them, poached in honey- and cinnamon-flavoured sherry.

INGREDIENTS 150 ml (¼ pint) clear honey │ 100 ml (3½ fl oz) sweet, dark sherry, such as Pedro Ximenez │ 1 teaspoon ground cinnamon │ 12 large dried figs │ 300 ml (½ pint) water │ 12 whole blanched almonds │ low-fat fromage frais or half-fat crème fraîche, to serve

ONE Put the honey, sherry, cinnamon, figs and measurement water in a saucepan over a medium-high heat and bring to the boil. Reduce the heat and simmer gently for 10–12 minutes. Remove from the heat and leave to stand, covered, for 3–4 hours. **TWO** Remove the figs from the pan with a slotted spoon, reserving the liquid. Bring the liquid to the boil over a high heat and boil for 4–5 minutes until thick and syrupy. Remove from the heat and set aside. **THREE** Using a small, sharp knife, make a small slit in the top of each fig and stuff it with an almond. Serve the figs drizzled with the warm syrup, with a dollop of fromage frais or crème fraîche.

Serves 4

NUTRIENT ANALYSIS PER SERVING 1366 kJ – 322 kcal – 4 g protein – 64 g carbohydrate – 64 g sugars – 5 g fat – 0 g saturates – 9 g fibre – 47 mg sodium

HEALTHY TIP Dried figs are a good source of dietary fibre, essential in helping the bowels work well and preventing constipation. Figs also contain useful amounts of calcium and magnesium, vital for the maintenance of bone tissue.

CINNAMON ICE CREAM

INGREDIENTS 750 ml (1¼ pints) vanilla-flavoured yogurt │ 2 tablespoons ground cinnamon │ 1 teaspoon finely grated lemon rind │ 4 tablespoons icing sugar │ sweet biscuits, to serve (optional)

ONE Mix all the ingredients together in a large bowl until well combined. Transfer the mixture to an ice-cream machine and churn until frozen, following the manufacturer's instructions. Transfer to a shallow freezerproof container and freeze until ready to use. **TWO** Alternatively, transfer to a shallow freezerproof container and freeze for 3–4 hours or until almost solid. Beat well with an electric whisk or transfer to a blender or food processor and blend until smooth, then return to the freezer. **THREE** Beat or blend in the same way after every 2 hours of freezing to break down all the ice crystals until the ice cream is smooth, then freeze again until solid. **FOUR** Transfer the ice cream to the refrigerator 20 minutes before serving. Scoop into chilled dessert glasses and serve with sweet biscuits, if desired.

Serves 4

NUTRIENT ANALYSIS PER SERVING 1056 kJ – 248 kcal – 7 g protein – 55 g carbohydrate – 55 g sugars – 2g fat – 1 g saturates – 0 g fibre – 120 mg sodium

HEALTHY TIP The yogurt used for this low-fat ice cream is an excellent source of calcium, magnesium and phosphorus. Calcium is essential for the maintenance of healthy bones.

ALMOND AND LEMON CAKE

This delightfully scented cake, flavoured with almonds and lemons, does not use any flour. It is particularly delicious served with a dollop of natural yogurt and fresh berries.

INGREDIENTS 4 eggs | 175 g (6 oz) golden caster sugar | finely grated rind and juice of 1 lemon | 400 g (13 oz) ground almonds | icing sugar, for dusting

ONE Grease a 20 cm (8 inch) square loose-bottomed cake tin and line the base with baking paper or greaseproof paper. **TWO** Beat the eggs with an electric whisk in a large bowl until pale and frothy. Gradually add the caster sugar and continue beating until pale and stiff. **THREE** Using a metal spoon, gently fold in the lemon rind and juice and the ground almonds until well combined. **FOUR** Spoon the cake mixture into the prepared tin and bake in a preheated oven, 190°C (375°F), Gas Mark 5, for 35–40 minutes or until browned and firm to touch, and a skewer inserted into the centre comes out clean. **FIVE** Transfer to a wire rack and leave to cool for 10 minutes before turning out. Remove and discard the lining paper. Dust with icing sugar before serving, cut into squares.

Serves 6

NUTRIENT ANALYSIS PER SERVING 2406 kJ – 577 kcal – 19 g protein – 35 g carbohydrate – 34 g sugars – 41 g fat – 4 g saturates – 9 g fibre – 60 mg sodium

HEALTHY TIP The almonds used in this cake make it quite high in dietary fibre. Eggs provide iron, as well as vitamins A and D. Most of our vitamin D is obtained by the action of daylight on skin, but eggs are one of the comparatively few dietary sources of the vitamin.

recipe illustrated on pages 242–243

BLOOD ORANGE ICE LOLLIES

The south coast of Valencia is known as the Costa del Azahar (coast of the orange blossom) and sailors are reputed to have been able to smell the fragrance of the native fruit up to ten nautical miles away. These ice lollies made with pure blood orange juice are so simple to prepare and really refreshing on a hot summer's day. Alternatively, you can use the juice of any ripe, fragrant oranges.

INGREDIENTS 500 ml (17 fl oz) freshly squeezed blood orange juice │ 2 tablespoons icing sugar

ONE Mix the blood orange juice and sugar together in a large jug. **TWO** Pour the juice mixture into 4 ice-lolly moulds and freeze for 3–4 hours or until solid. **THREE** When ready to serve, dip the lolly moulds in hot water for 20–30 seconds, then pop the lollies out. Serve immediately.

Serves 4

NUTRIENT ANALYSIS PER SERVING 300 kJ – 70 kcal – 1 g protein – 18 g carbohydrate – 18 g sugars – 0 g fat – 0 g saturates – 0 g fibre – 3 mg sodium

HEALTHY TIP Orange juice is a particularly good source of vitamin C, an essential antioxidant and vital for the protection and maintenance of body tissue. Oranges are also high in carotenes, which are thought to have an important role in protecting against cancer.

recipe illustrated on pages 246–247

ALMOND MILK

This sumptuously creamy almond drink is to be found all over juice bars and ice-cream parlours in Spain. It is also available in cartons from grocery stores and supermarkets. Use the finest-quality Spanish almonds for this refreshing and nutritious drink.

INGREDIENTS 300 g (10 oz) whole blanched almonds | 1.5 litres (2½ pints) water | 2 tablespoons golden caster sugar | pinch of ground cinnamon | crushed ice, to serve

ONE Put the almonds in a food processor with 400 ml (14 fl oz) of the measurement water and process until as smooth as possible. **TWO** Transfer to a bowl with the remaining water and stir well. Cover and leave to infuse overnight in the refrigerator. **THREE** Strain the liquid through a very fine muslin cloth into a saucepan and add the sugar and cinnamon. Bring the mixture to the boil, then remove from the heat and leave to cool. Transfer to a jug or bowl, cover and chill in the refrigerator for 3–4 hours. **FOUR** When ready to serve, fill 4 tall glasses with crushed ice, pour the almond milk over and serve immediately.

Serves 4

NUTRIENT ANALYSIS PER SERVING 1118 kJ – 269 kcal – 8 g protein – 13 g carbohydrate – 12 g sugars – 21 g fat – 2 g saturates – 0 g fibre – 11 mg sodium

HEALTHY TIP Almonds, like most nuts, are a great way of consuming vitamin E, which is a valuable antioxidant. They also contain useful amounts of the B vitamins and are quite a good source of calcium, magnesium and phosphorus.

SPARKLING PEACH SANGRIA

INGREDIENTS 4 ripe peaches, skinned *(see page 230)*, stoned and sliced | 25 g (1 oz) golden caster sugar | 5 tablespoons peach-flavoured liqueur | 1 small lemon, halved and thinly sliced | 200 ml (7 fl oz) peach juice | 750 ml (1¼ pints) chilled cava or any other sparkling dry white wine | ice cubes or crushed ice, to serve

ONE Put the peaches, sugar, liqueur, lemon slices and peach juice in a bowl. Cover and chill overnight in the refrigerator. **TWO** When ready to serve, fill 6 tall, chilled glasses with ice. Transfer the peach mixture to a large jug or bowl. Pour over the cava or other sparkling white wine, stir and pour into the prepared glasses, spooning some of the sliced fruit into each one. Serve immediately.

Serves 6

NUTRIENT ANALYSIS PER SERVING 1169 kJ – 277 kcal – 2 g protein – 30 g carbohydrate – 30 g sugars – 0 g fat – 0 g saturates – 3 g fibre – 16 mg sodium

HEALTHY TIP The peach juice in this drink contains vitamins B and C, as well as carotene, the precursor to vitamin A. Bear in mind that the alcohol in sparkling wine is absorbed into the bloodstream more quickly than that in still wine – enjoy it slowly!

INDEX

ACKNOWLEDGEMENTS

EXECUTIVE EDITOR Nicky Hill

EDITOR Emma Pattison

EXECUTIVE ART EDITOR Joanna MacGregor

SENIOR PRODUCTION CONTROLLER Martin Croshaw

PHOTOGRAPHY Jason Lowe/© Octopus Publishing

FOOD STYLIST Sunil Vijayakar

PROPS STYLIST Liz Hippisley